PASSION
OF THE AGES

E.G. WHITE

HOMEWARD PUBLISHING

PASSION OF THE AGES

© 2004 by HOMEWARD PUBLISHING
First Printing, February 2004
Second Printing, March 2004

Cover and book design - CherryDeZign

Cover art - Jimi Claybrooks

Cover portrait of Jesus - Sharon Zeismer

Published by
HOMEWARD PUBLISHING
P.O. Box111
Earlton, New York 12058
1-800-823-0481

www.passionoftheages.com
E-mail: shorter@mhonline.net

ISBN-0-938805-07-X

Printed by Review & Herald Graphics

THE REAL PASSION PLAY

el Gibson's, "Passion of the Christ," touches a vital nerve. For many it is a deeply moving spiritual experience. For others the violent portrayal of Christ's brutal suffering is too great for them to emotionally handle.

Perhaps you have seen the film or maybe you haven't. What's the meaning of it all? Why all this horror? Was Jesus simply a martyr dying for a good cause? Why is the cross at the heart of Christianity?

There is something beyond the excruciating pain Jesus experienced on the cross. There is something more significant than the immensity of His physical suffering. There is something more than strong-armed, muscular Roman soldiers driving jagged nails through tender flesh. There is something more than a Roman lash embedded with fragments of metal ripping out hunks of flesh from His lacerated back. As horrible as His physical suffering really was, if that is all we see happening on Golgotha's mountain we have really missed the meaning of it all. . .

Mark A Finley
World Evangelist
It Is Written Television
Simi Valley, California

For the complete "The Real Passion Play", see page 149.

INTRODUCTION

Faith is not an opiate, but a stimulant. Looking to Calvary will not quiet your soul into non-performance of duty, but will create faith that will work, purifying the soul from all selfishness.

"The faith in Christ which saves the soul is not what is represented to be by many. "Believe, Believe," is their cry; "only believe in Christ, and you will be saved. It is all you have to do." While true faith trusts wholly in Christ for salvation, it will lead to perfect conformity to the law of God."

E.G. White

CONTENTS

Lest I forget Gethsemane,

Lest I forget Thine agony,

Lest I forget Thy love for me,

Lead me to Calvary

—Jennie E. Hussey

ONE

GETHSEMANE

In company with His disciples, the Saviour slowly made His way to the garden of Gethsemane. The Passover moon, broad and full, shone from a cloudless sky. The city of pilgrims' tents was hushed into silence.

Jesus had been earnestly conversing with His disciples and instructing them; but as He neared Gethsemane, He became strangely silent. He had often visited this spot for meditation and prayer; but never with a heart so full of sorrow as upon this night of His last agony. Throughout His life on earth He had walked in the light of God's presence. When in conflict with men who were inspired by the very spirit of Satan, He could say, "He that sent Me is with Me: the Father hath not left Me alone; for I do always those things that please Him." John 8:29. But now He seemed to be shut out from the light of God's sustaining presence. Now He was numbered with the transgressors. The guilt of fallen humanity He must bear. Upon Him who knew no sin must be laid the iniquity of us all. So dreadful does sin appear to Him, so great is the weight of guilt which He must bear, that He is tempted to fear it will shut Him out forever from His Father's love. Feeling how terrible is the wrath of God against transgression, He exclaims, "My soul is exceeding sorrowful, even unto death."

As they approached the garden, the disciples had marked the change that came over their Master. Never before had they seen Him so utterly sad and silent. As He proceeded, this strange sadness deepened; yet they dared not question Him as to the cause. His form swayed as if He were about to fall. Upon reaching the garden, the disciples looked anxiously for His usual place of retirement, that their

7

Master might rest. Every step that He now took was with labored effort. He groaned aloud, as if suffering under the pressure of a terrible burden. Twice His companions supported Him, or He would have fallen to the earth.

Near the entrance to the garden, Jesus left all but three of the disciples, bidding them pray for themselves and for Him. With Peter, James, and John, He entered its secluded recesses. These three disciples were Christ's closest companions. They had beheld His glory on the mount of transfiguration; they had seen Moses and Elijah talking with Him; they had heard the voice from heaven; now in His great struggle, Christ desired their presence near Him. Often they had passed the night with Him in this retreat. On these occasions, after a season of watching and prayer, they would sleep undisturbed at a little distance from their Master, until He awoke them in the morning to go forth anew to labor. But now He desired them to spend the night with Him in prayer. Yet He could not bear that even they should witness the agony He was to endure.

"Tarry ye here," He said, "and watch with Me." He went a little distance from them—not so far but that they could both see and hear Him—and fell prostrate upon the ground. He felt that by sin He was being separated from His Father. The gulf was so broad, so black, so deep, that His spirit shuddered before it. This agony He must not exert His divine power to escape. As man He must suffer the consequences of man's sin. As man He must endure the wrath of God against transgression.

Christ was now standing in a different attitude from that in which He had ever stood before. His suffering can best be described in the words of the prophet, "Awake, O sword, against My shepherd, and against the man that is My fellow, saith the Lord of hosts." Zech. 13:7. As the substitute and surety for sinful man, Christ was suffering under divine justice. He saw what justice meant. Hitherto He had been as an intercessor for others; now He longed to have an intercessor for Himself.

As Christ felt His unity with the Father broken up, He feared that in His human nature He would be unable to endure the coming conflict with the powers of darkness. In the wilderness of temptation the destiny of the human race had been at stake. Christ was then conqueror. Now the tempter had come for the last fearful struggle. For this he had been preparing during the three years of Christ's ministry. Everything was at stake with him. If he failed here, his hope of mastery was lost; the kingdoms of the world would finally become Christ's; he himself would be overthrown and cast out. But if Christ could be overcome, the earth would become Satan's kingdom, and the human race would be forever in his power. With the issues of the conflict before Him, Christ's soul was filled with dread of separation from God. Satan told Him that if He became the surety for a sinful world, the separation would be eternal. He would be identified with Satan's kingdom, and would nevermore be one with God.

And what was to be gained by this sacrifice? How hopeless appeared the guilt and ingratitude of men! In its hardest features Satan pressed the situation upon the Redeemer: The people who claim to be above all others in temporal and spiritual advantages have rejected You. They are seeking to destroy You, the foundation, the center and seal of the promises made to them as a peculiar people. One of Your own disciples, who has listened to Your instruction, and has been among the foremost in church activities, will betray You. One of Your most zealous followers will deny You. All will forsake You. Christ's whole being abhorred the thought. That those whom He had undertaken to save, those whom He loved so much, should unite in the plots of Satan, this pierced His soul. The conflict was terrible. Its measure was the guilt of His nation, of His accusers and betrayer, the guilt of a world lying in wickedness. The sins of men weighed heavily upon Christ, and the sense of God's wrath against sin was crushing out His life.

Behold Him contemplating the price to be paid for the human soul. In His agony He clings to the cold ground, as if to prevent Himself from being drawn farther from God. The chilling dew of night falls upon His prostrate form, but He heeds it not. From His pale lips comes the bitter cry, "O My Father, if it be possible, let this cup pass from Me." Yet even now He adds, "Nevertheless not as I will, but as Thou wilt."

The human heart longs for sympathy in suffering. This longing Christ felt to the very depths of His being. In the supreme agony of His soul He came to His disciples with a yearning desire to hear some words of comfort from those whom He had so often blessed and comforted, and shielded in sorrow and distress. The One who had always had words of sympathy for them was now suffering superhuman agony, and He longed to know that they were praying for Him and for themselves. How dark seemed the malignity of sin! Terrible was the temptation to let the human race bear the consequences of its own guilt, while He stood innocent before God. If He could only know that His disciples understood and appreciated this, He would be strengthened.

Rising with painful effort, He staggered to the place where He had left His companions. But He "findeth them asleep." Had He found them praying, He would have been relieved. Had they been seeking refuge in God, that satanic agencies might not prevail over them, He would have been comforted by their steadfast faith. But they had not heeded the repeated warning, "Watch and pray." At first they had been much troubled to see their Master, usually so calm and dignified, wrestling with a sorrow that was beyond comprehension. They had prayed as they heard the strong cries of the sufferer. They did not intend to forsake their Lord, but they seemed paralyzed by a stupor which they might have shaken off if they had continued pleading with God. They did not realize the necessity of watchfulness and earnest prayer in order to withstand temptation.

Just before He bent His footsteps to the garden, Jesus had said to the disciples, "All ye shall be offended because of Me this night." They had given Him the strongest assurance that they would go with Him to prison and to death. And poor, self-sufficient Peter had added, "Although all shall be offended, yet will not I." Mark 14:27, 29. But the disciples trusted to themselves. They did not look to the mighty

Helper as Christ had counseled them to do. Thus when the Saviour was most in need of their sympathy and prayers, they were found asleep. Even Peter was sleeping.

And John, the loving disciple who had leaned upon the breast of Jesus, was asleep. Surely, the love of John for his Master should have kept him awake. His earnest prayers should have mingled with those of his loved Saviour in the time of His supreme sorrow. The Redeemer had spent entire nights praying for His disciples, that their faith might not fail. Should Jesus now put to James and John the question He had once asked them, "Are ye able to drink of the cup that I shall drink of, and to be baptized with the baptism that I am baptized with?" they would not have ventured to answer, "We are able." Matt. 20:22.

The disciples awakened at the voice of Jesus, but they hardly knew Him, His face was so changed by anguish. Addressing Peter, Jesus said, "Simon, sleepest thou? couldest not thou watch one hour? Watch ye and pray, lest ye enter into temptation. The spirit truly is ready, but the flesh is weak." The weakness of His disciples awakened the sympathy of Jesus. He feared that they would not be able to endure the test which would come upon them in His betrayal and death. He did not reprove them, but said, "Watch ye and pray, lest ye enter into temptation." Even in His great agony, He was seeking to excuse their weakness. "The spirit truly is ready," He said, "but the flesh is weak."

Again the Son of God was seized with superhuman agony, and fainting and exhausted, He staggered back to the place of His former struggle. His suffering was even greater than before. As the agony of soul came upon Him, "His sweat was as it were great drops of blood falling down to the ground." The cypress and palm trees were the silent witnesses of His anguish. From their leafy branches dropped heavy dew upon His stricken form, as if nature wept over its Author wrestling alone with the powers of darkness.

A short time before, Jesus had stood like a mighty cedar, withstanding the storm of opposition that spent its fury upon Him. Stubborn wills, and hearts filled with malice and subtlety, had striven in vain to confuse and overpower Him. He stood forth in divine majesty as the Son of God. Now He was like a reed beaten and bent by the angry storm. He had approached the consummation of His work a conqueror, having at each step gained the victory over the powers of darkness. As one already glorified, He had claimed oneness with God. In unfaltering accents He had poured out His songs of praise. He had spoken to His disciples in words of courage and tenderness. Now had come the hour of the power of darkness. Now His voice was heard on the still evening air, not in tones of triumph, but full of human anguish. The words of the Saviour were borne to the ears of the drowsy disciples, "O My Father, if this cup may not pass away from Me, except I drink it, Thy will be done."

The first impulse of the disciples was to go to Him; but He had bidden them tarry there, watching unto prayer. When Jesus came to them, He found them still sleeping. Again He had felt a longing for companionship, for some words from His disciples which would bring relief, and break the spell of darkness that well-nigh overpowered Him. But their eyes were heavy; "neither wist they what to answer Him." His presence aroused them. They saw His face marked with the bloody sweat of agony, and they were filled with fear. His anguish of mind they could not understand. "His visage was so marred more than any man, and His form more than the sons of men." Isa. 52:14.

Turning away, Jesus sought again His retreat, and fell prostrate, overcome by the horror of a great darkness. The humanity of the Son of God trembled in that trying hour. He prayed not now for His disciples that their faith might not fail, but for His own tempted, agonized soul. The awful moment had come—that moment which was to decide the destiny of the world. The fate of humanity trembled in the balance. Christ might even now refuse to drink the cup apportioned to guilty man. It was not yet too late. He might wipe the bloody sweat from His brow, and leave man to perish in his iniquity. He might say, Let the transgressor receive the penalty of his sin, and I will go back to My Father. Will the Son of God drink the bitter cup of humiliation and agony? Will the innocent suffer the consequences of the curse of sin, to save the guilty? The words fall tremblingly from the pale lips of Jesus, "O My Father, if this cup may not pass away from Me, except I drink it, Thy will be done."

Three times has He uttered that prayer. Three times has humanity shrunk from the last, crowning sacrifice. But now the history of the human race comes up before the world's Redeemer. He sees that the transgressors of the law, if left to themselves, must perish. He sees the helplessness of man. He sees the power of sin. The woes and lamentations of a doomed world rise before Him. He beholds its impending fate, and His decision is made. He will save man at any cost to Himself. He accepts His baptism of blood, that through Him perishing millions may gain everlasting life. He has left the courts of heaven, where all is purity, happiness, and glory, to save the one lost sheep, the one world that has fallen by transgression. And He will not turn from His mission. He will become the propitiation of a race that has willed to sin. His prayer now breathes only submission: "If this cup may not pass away from Me, except I drink it, Thy will be done."

Having made the decision, He fell dying to the ground from which He had partially risen. Where now were His disciples, to place their hands tenderly beneath the head of their fainting Master, and bathe that brow, marred indeed more than the sons of men? The Saviour trod the wine press alone, and of the people there was none with Him.

But God suffered with His Son. Angels beheld the Saviour's agony. They saw their Lord enclosed by legions of satanic forces, His nature weighed down with a shuddering, mysterious dread. There was silence in heaven. No harp was touched. Could mortals have viewed the amazement of the angelic host as in silent grief they watched the Father separating His beams of light, love, and glory from His beloved Son, they would better understand how offensive in His sight is sin.

The worlds unfallen and the heavenly angels had watched with intense interest as the conflict drew to its close. Satan and his confederacy of evil, the legions of apostasy, watched intently this great crisis in the work of redemption. The powers of good and evil waited to see what answer would come to Christ's thrice-repeated prayer. Angels had longed to bring relief to the divine sufferer, but this might not be. No way of escape was found for the Son of God. In this awful crisis, when everything was at stake, when the mysterious cup trembled in the hand of the sufferer, the heavens opened, a light shone forth amid the stormy darkness of the crisis hour, and the mighty angel who stands in God's presence, occupying the position from which Satan fell, came to the side of Christ. The angel came not to take the cup from Christ's hand, but to strengthen Him to drink it, with the assurance of the Father's love. He came to give power to the divine-human suppliant. He pointed Him to the open heavens, telling Him of the souls that would be saved as the result of His sufferings. He assured Him that His Father is greater and more powerful than Satan, that His death would result in the utter discomfiture of Satan, and that the kingdom of this world would be given to the saints of the Most High. He told Him that He would see of the travail of His soul, and be satisfied, for He would see a multitude of the human race saved, eternally saved.

Christ's agony did not cease, but His depression and discouragement left Him. The storm had in nowise abated, but He who was its object was strengthened to meet its fury. He came forth calm and serene. A heavenly peace rested upon His bloodstained face. He had borne that which no human being could ever bear; for He had tasted the sufferings of death for every man.

The sleeping disciples had been suddenly awakened by the light surrounding the Saviour. They saw the angel bending over their prostrate Master. They saw him lift the Saviour's head upon his bosom, and point toward heaven. They heard his voice, like sweetest music, speaking words of comfort and hope. The disciples recalled the scene upon the mount of transfiguration. They remembered the glory that in the temple had encircled Jesus, and the voice of God that spoke from the cloud. Now that same glory was again revealed, and they had no further fear for their Master. He was under the care of God; a mighty angel had been sent to protect Him. Again the disciples in their weariness yield to the strange stupor that overpowers them.

Again Jesus finds them sleeping.

Looking sorrowfully upon them He says, "Sleep on now, and take your rest: behold, the hour is at hand, and the Son of man is betrayed into the hands of sinners."

Even as He spoke these words, He heard the footsteps of the mob in search of Him, and said, "Rise, let us be going: behold, he is at hand that doth betray Me."

No traces of His recent agony were visible as Jesus stepped forth to meet His betrayer. Standing in advance of His disciples He said, "Whom seek ye?" They answered, "Jesus of Nazareth." Jesus replied, "I am He." As these words were spoken, the angel who had lately ministered to Jesus moved between Him and the mob. A divine light illuminated the Saviour's face, and a dovelike form overshadowed Him. In the presence of this divine glory, the murderous throng could not stand for a moment. They staggered back. Priests, elders, soldiers, and even Judas, fell as dead men to the ground.

The angel withdrew, and the light faded away. Jesus had opportunity to escape, but He remained, calm and self-possessed. As one glorified He stood in the midst of that hardened band, now prostrate and helpless at His feet. The disciples looked on, silent with wonder and awe.

But quickly the scene changed. The mob started up. The Roman soldiers, the priests and Judas, gathered about Christ. They seemed ashamed of their weakness, and fearful that He would yet escape. Again the question was asked by the Redeemer, "Whom seek ye?" They had had evidence that He who stood before them was the Son of God, but they would not be convinced. To the question, "Whom seek ye?" again they answered, "Jesus of Nazareth." The Saviour then said, "I have told you that I am He: if therefore ye seek Me, let these go their way"—pointing to the disciples. He knew how weak was their faith, and He sought to shield them from temptation and trial. For them He was ready to sacrifice Himself.

Judas the betrayer did not forget the part he was to act. When the mob entered the garden, he had led the way, closely followed by the high priest. To the pursuers of Jesus he had given a sign, saying, "Whomsoever I shall kiss, that same is He: hold Him fast." Matt. 26:48. Now he pretends to have no part with them. Coming close to Jesus, he takes His hand as a familiar friend. With the words, "Hail, Master," he kisses Him repeatedly, and appears to weep as if in sympathy with Him in His peril.

Jesus said to him, "Friend, wherefore art thou come?" His voice trembled with sorrow as He added, "Judas, betrayest thou the Son of man with a kiss?" This appeal should have aroused the conscience of the betrayer, and touched his stubborn heart; but honor, fidelity, and human tenderness had forsaken him. He stood bold and defiant, showing no disposition to relent. He had given himself up to Satan, and he had no power to resist him. Jesus did not refuse the traitor's kiss.

The mob grew bold as they saw Judas touch the person of Him who had so recently been glorified before their eyes. They now laid hold of Jesus, and proceeded to bind those precious hands that had ever been employed in doing good.

The disciples had thought that their Master would not suffer Himself to be taken. For the same power that had caused the mob to fall as dead men could keep them helpless, until Jesus and His companions should escape. They were disappointed and indignant as they saw the cords brought forward to bind the hands of Him whom they loved. Peter in his anger rashly drew his sword and tried to defend his Master, but he only cut off an ear of the high priest's servant. When Jesus saw what was done, He released His hands, though held firmly by the Roman soldiers, and saying, "Suffer ye thus far," He touched the wounded ear, and it was instantly made whole. He then said to Peter, "Put up again thy sword into his place: for all they that take the sword shall perish with the sword. Thinkest thou that I cannot now pray to My Father, and He shall presently give Me more than twelve legions of angels?"—a legion in place of each one of the disciples. Oh, why, the disciples thought, does He not save Himself and us? Answering their unspoken thought, He added, "But how then shall the scriptures be fulfilled, that thus it must be?" "The cup which My Father hath given Me, shall I not drink it?"

The official dignity of the Jewish leaders had not prevented them from joining in the pursuit of Jesus. His arrest was too important a matter to be trusted to subordinates; the wily priests and elders had joined the temple police and the rabble in following Judas to Gethsemane. What a company for those dignitaries to unite with—a mob that was eager for excitement, and armed with all kinds of implements, as if in pursuit of a wild beast!

Turning to the priests and elders, Christ fixed upon them His searching glance. The words He spoke they would never forget as long as life should last. They were as the sharp arrows of the Almighty. With dignity He said: You come out against Me with swords and staves as you would against a thief or a robber. Day by day I sat teaching in the temple. You had every opportunity of laying hands upon Me, and you did nothing. The night is better suited to your work. "This is your hour, and the power of darkness."

The disciples were terrified as they saw Jesus permit Himself to be taken and bound. They were offended that He should suffer this humiliation to Himself and them. They could not understand His conduct, and they blamed Him for submitting to the mob. In their indignation and fear, Peter proposed that they save themselves. Following this suggestion, "they all forsook Him, and fled." But Christ had foretold this desertion, "Behold," He had said, "the hour cometh, yea, is now come, that ye shall be scattered, every man to his own, and shall leave Me alone: and yet I am not alone, because the Father is with Me." John 16:32.

TWO

BEFORE ANNAS AND THE COURT OF CAIAPHAS

Over the brook Kedron, past gardens and olive groves, and through the hushed streets of the sleeping city, they hurried Jesus. It was past midnight, and the cries of the hooting mob that followed Him broke sharply upon the still air. The Saviour was bound and closely guarded, and He moved painfully. But in eager haste His captors made their way with Him to the palace of Annas, the ex-high priest.

Annas was the head of the officiating priestly family, and in deference to his age he was recognized by the people as high priest. His counsel was sought and carried out as the voice of God. He must first see Jesus a captive to priestly power. He must be present at the examination of the prisoner, for fear that the less-experienced Caiaphas might fail of securing the object for which they were working. His artifice, cunning, and subtlety must be used on this occasion; for, at all events, Christ's condemnation must be secured.

Christ was to be tried formally before the Sanhedrin; but before Annas He was subjected to a preliminary trial. Under the Roman rule the Sanhedrin could not execute the sentence of death. They could only examine a prisoner, and pass judgment, to be ratified by the Roman authorities. It was therefore necessary to bring against Christ charges that would be regarded as criminal by the Romans. An accusation must also be found which would condemn Him in the eyes of the Jews. Not a few among the priests and rulers had been convicted by Christ's teaching, and only fear of excommunication prevented them from confessing Him. The priests well remembered the question of Nicodemus, "Doth our law judge any man, before it hear him, and know what he doeth?" John 7:51. This question had for the time broken up the council, and thwarted their plans. Joseph of Arimathaea and Nicodemus were not now to be summoned, but there were others who might dare to speak in favor of justice. The trial must be so conducted as to unite the members of the Sanhedrin against Christ. There were two charges which the priests desired to maintain. If Jesus could be proved a blasphemer, He would be condemned by the Jews. If convicted of sedition, it would secure His condemnation by the Romans. The second charge Annas tried first to establish. He questioned Jesus concerning His disciples and His doctrines, hoping the prisoner would say something that would give him material upon which to work. He thought to draw out some statement to prove that He was seeking to establish a secret society, with the purpose of setting up a new kingdom. Then the priests could deliver Him to the Romans as a disturber of the peace and a creator of insurrection.

Christ read the priest's purpose as an open book. As if reading the inmost soul of His questioner, He denied that there was between Him and His followers any secret bond of union, or that He gathered them secretly and in the darkness to conceal His designs. He had no secrets in regard to His purposes or doctrines. "I spake openly to the world," He answered; "I ever taught in the synagogue, and in the temple, whither the Jews always resort; and in secret have I said nothing."

The Saviour contrasted His own manner of work with the methods of His accusers. For months they had hunted Him, striving to entrap Him and bring Him before a secret tribunal, where they might obtain by perjury what it was impossible to gain by fair means. Now they were carrying out their purpose. The midnight seizure by a mob, the mockery and abuse before He was condemned, or even accused, was their manner of work, not His. Their action was in violation of the law. Their own rules declared that every man should be treated as innocent until proved guilty. By their own rules the priests stood condemned.

Turning upon His questioner, Jesus said, "Why askest thou Me?" Had not the priests and rulers sent spies to watch His movements, and report His every word? Had not these been present at every gathering of the people, and carried to the priests information of all His sayings and doings? "Ask them which heard Me, what I have said unto them," replied Jesus; "behold, they know what I said."

Annas was silenced by the decision of the answer. Fearing that Christ would say something regarding his course of action that he would prefer to keep covered up, he said nothing more to Him at this time. One of his officers, filled with wrath as he saw Annas silenced, struck Jesus on the face, saying, "Answerest Thou the high priest so?"

Christ calmly replied, "If I have spoken evil, bear witness of the evil: but if well, why smitest thou Me?" He spoke no burning words of retaliation. His calm answer came from a heart sinless, patient, and gentle, that would not be provoked.

Christ suffered keenly under abuse and insult. At the hands of the beings whom He had created, and for whom He was making an infinite sacrifice, He received every indignity. And He suffered in proportion to the perfection of His holiness and His hatred of sin. His trial by men who acted as fiends was to Him a perpetual sacrifice. To be surrounded by human beings under the control of Satan was revolting to Him. And He knew that in a moment, by the flashing forth of His divine power, He could lay His cruel tormentors in the dust. This made the trial the harder to bear.

The Jews were looking for a Messiah to be revealed in outward show. They expected Him, by one flash of overmastering will, to change the current of men's thoughts, and force from them an acknowledgment of His supremacy. Thus, they believed, He was to secure His own exaltation, and gratify their ambitious hopes. Thus when Christ was treated with contempt, there came to Him a strong temptation to manifest His divine character. By a word, by a look, He could compel His persecutors to confess that He was Lord above kings and rulers, priests and temple. But it was His difficult task to keep to the position He had chosen as one with humanity.

The angels of heaven witnessed every movement made against their loved Commander. They longed to deliver Christ. Under God the angels are all-powerful. On one occasion, in obedience to the command of Christ, they slew of the Assyrian army in one night one hundred and eighty-five thousand men. How easily could the angels, beholding the shameful scene of the trial of Christ, have testified their indignation by consuming the adversaries of God! But they were not commanded to do this. He who could have doomed His enemies to death bore with their cruelty. His love for His Father, and His pledge, made from the foundation of the world, to become the Sin Bearer, led Him to endure uncomplainingly the coarse treatment of those He came to save. It was a part of His mission to bear, in His humanity, all the taunts and abuse that men could heap upon Him. The only hope of humanity was in this submission of Christ to all that He could endure from the hands and hearts of men.

Christ had said nothing that could give His accusers an advantage; yet He was bound, to signify that He was condemned. There must, however, be a pretense of justice. It was necessary that there should be the form of a legal trial. This the authorities were determined to hasten. They knew the regard in which Jesus was held by the people, and feared that if the arrest were noised abroad, a rescue would be attempted. Again, if the trial and execution were not brought about at once, there would be a week's delay on account of the celebration of the Passover. This might defeat their plans. In securing the condemnation of Jesus they depended largely upon the clamor of the mob, many of them the rabble of Jerusalem. Should there be a week's delay, the excitement would abate, and a reaction would be likely to set in. The better part of the people would be aroused in Christ's favor; many would come forward with testimony in His vindication, bringing to light the mighty works He had done. This would excite popular indignation against the Sanhedrin. Their proceedings would be condemned, and Jesus would be set free, to receive new homage from the multitudes. The priests and rulers therefore determined that before their purpose could become known, Jesus should be delivered into the hands of the Romans.

But first of all, an accusation was to be found. They had gained nothing as yet. Annas ordered Jesus to be taken to Caiaphas. Caiaphas belonged to the Sadducees, some of whom were now the most desperate enemies of Jesus. He himself, though wanting in force of character, was fully as severe, heartless, and unscrupulous as was Annas. He would leave no means untried to destroy Jesus. It was now early morning, and very dark; by the light of torches and lanterns the armed band with their prisoner proceeded to the high priest's palace. Here, while the members of the Sanhedrin were coming together, Annas and Caiaphas again questioned Jesus, but without success.

When the council had assembled in the judgment hall, Caiaphas took his seat as presiding officer. On either side were the judges, and those specially interested in the trial. The Roman soldiers were stationed on the platform below the throne. At the foot of the throne stood Jesus. Upon Him the gaze of the whole multitude was fixed. The excitement was intense. Of all the throng He alone was calm and serene. The very atmosphere surrounding Him seemed pervaded by a holy influence.

Caiaphas had regarded Jesus as his rival. The eagerness of the people to hear the Saviour, and their apparent readiness to accept His teachings, had aroused the bitter jealousy of the high priest. But as Caiaphas now looked upon the prisoner, he was struck with admiration for His noble and dignified bearing. A conviction came over him that this Man was akin to God. The next instant he scornfully banished the thought. Immediately his voice was heard in sneering, haughty tones demanding that Jesus work one of His mighty miracles before them. But his words fell upon the Saviour's ears as though He heard them not. The people compared the excited and malignant deportment of Annas and Caiaphas with the calm, majestic bearing of Jesus. Even in the minds of that hardened multitude arose the question, Is this man of godlike presence to be condemned as a criminal?

Caiaphas, perceiving the influence that was obtaining, hastened the trial. The enemies of Jesus were in great perplexity. They were bent on securing His condemnation, but how to accomplish this they knew not. The members of the council were divided between the Pharisees and the Sadducees. There was bitter animosity and controversy between them; certain disputed points they dared not approach for fear of a quarrel. With a few words Jesus could have excited their prejudices against each other, and thus have averted their wrath from Himself. Caiaphas knew this, and he wished to avoid stirring up a contention. There were plenty of witnesses to prove that Christ had denounced the priests and scribes, that He had called them hypocrites and murderers; but this testimony it was not expedient to bring forward. The Sadducees in their sharp contentions with the Pharisees had used to them similar language. And such testimony would have no weight with the Romans, who were themselves disgusted with the pretensions of the Pharisees. There was abundant evidence that Jesus had disregarded the traditions of the Jews, and had spoken irreverently of many of their ordinances; but in regard to tradition the Pharisees and Sadducees were at swords' points; and this evidence also would have no weight with the Romans. Christ's enemies dared not accuse Him of Sabbathbreaking, lest an examination should reveal the character of His work. If His miracles of healing were brought to light, the very object of the priests would be defeated.

False witnesses had been bribed to accuse Jesus of inciting rebellion and seeking to establish a separate government. But their testimony proved to be vague and contradictory. Under examination they falsified their own statements.

Early in His ministry Christ had said, "Destroy this temple, and in three days I will raise it up." In the figurative language of prophecy, He had thus foretold His own death and resurrection. "He spake of the temple of His body." John 2:19, 21. These words the Jews had understood in a literal sense, as referring to the temple at Jerusalem. Of all that Christ had said, the priests could find nothing to use against Him save this. By misstating these words they hoped to gain an advantage. The Romans had engaged in rebuilding and embellishing the temple, and they took great pride in it; any contempt shown to it would be sure to excite their indignation. Here Romans and Jews, Pharisees and Sadducees, could meet; for all held the temple in great veneration. On this point two witnesses were found whose testimony was not so contradictory as that of the others had been. One of them, who had been bribed to accuse Jesus, declared, "This fellow said, I am able to destroy the temple of God, and to build it in three days." Thus Christ's words were misstated. If they had been reported exactly as He spoke them, they would not have secured His condemnation even by the Sanhedrin. Had Jesus been a mere man, as the Jews claimed, His declaration would only have indicated an unreasonable, boastful spirit, but could not have been construed into blasphemy. Even as misrepresented by the false witnesses, His words contained nothing which would be regarded by the Romans as a crime worthy of death.

Patiently Jesus listened to the conflicting testimonies. No word did He utter in self-defense. At last His accusers were entangled, confused, and maddened. The trial was making no headway; it seemed that their plottings were to fail. Caiaphas was desperate. One last resort remained; Christ must be forced to condemn Himself. The high priest started from the judgment seat, his face contorted with passion, his voice and demeanor plainly indicating that were it in his power he would strike down the prisoner before him. "Answerest Thou nothing?" he exclaimed; "what is it which these witness against Thee?"

Jesus held His peace. "He was oppressed, and He was afflicted, yet He opened not His mouth: He is brought as a lamb to the slaughter, and as a sheep before her shearers is dumb, so He openeth not His mouth." Isaiah 53:7.

At last, Caiaphas, raising his right hand toward heaven, addressed Jesus in the form of a solemn oath: "I adjure Thee by the living God, that Thou tell us whether Thou be the Christ, the Son of God."

To this appeal Christ could not remain silent. There was a time to be silent, and a time to speak. He had not spoken until directly questioned. He knew that to answer now would make His death certain. But the appeal was made by the highest acknowledged authority of the nation, and in the name of the Most High. Christ would not fail to show proper respect for the law. More than this, His own relation to the Father was called in question. He must plainly declare His character and mission. Jesus had said to His disciples, "Whosoever therefore shall confess Me before men, him will I confess also before My Father which is in heaven." Matt. 10:32. Now by His own example He repeated the lesson.

Every ear was bent to listen, and every eye was fixed on His face as He answered, "Thou hast said." A heavenly light seemed to illuminate His pale countenance as He added, "Nevertheless I say unto you, Hereafter shall ye see the Son of man sitting on the right hand of power, and coming in the clouds of heaven."

For a moment the divinity of Christ flashed through His guise of humanity. The high priest quailed before the penetrating eyes of the Saviour. That look seemed to read his hidden thoughts, and burn into his heart. Never in afterlife did he forget that searching glance of the persecuted Son of God.

"Hereafter," said Jesus, "shall ye see the Son of man sitting on the right hand of power, and coming in the clouds of heaven." In these words Christ presented the reverse of the scene then taking place. He, the Lord of life and glory, would be seated at God's right hand. He would be the judge of all the earth, and from His decision there could be no appeal. Then every secret thing would be set in the light of God's countenance, and judgment be passed upon every man according to his deeds.

The words of Christ startled the high priest. The thought that there was to be a resurrection of the dead, when all would stand at the bar of God, to be rewarded according to their works, was a thought of terror to Caiaphas. He did not wish to believe that in future he would receive sentence according to his works. There rushed before his mind as a panorama the scenes of the final judgment. For a moment he saw the fearful spectacle of the graves giving up their dead, with the secrets he had hoped were forever hidden. For a moment he felt as if standing before the eternal Judge, whose eye, which sees all things, was reading his soul, bringing to light mysteries supposed to be hidden with the dead.

The scene passed from the priest's vision. Christ's words cut him, the Sadducee, to the quick. Caiaphas had denied the doctrine of the resurrection, the judgment, and a future life. Now he was maddened by satanic fury. Was this man, a prisoner before him, to assail his most cherished theories? Rending his robe, that the people might see his pretended horror, he demanded that without further preliminaries the prisoner be condemned for blasphemy. "What further need have we of witnesses?" he said; "behold, now ye have heard His blasphemy. What think ye?" And they all condemned Him.

Conviction mingled with passion led Caiaphas to do as he did. He was furious with himself for believing Christ's words, and instead of rending his heart under a deep sense of truth, and confessing that Jesus was the Messiah, he rent his priestly robes in determined resistance. This act was deeply significant. Little did Caiaphas realize its meaning. In this act, done to influence the judges and secure Christ's condemnation, the high priest had condemned himself. By the law of God he was disqualified for the priesthood. He had pronounced upon himself the death sentence.

A high priest was not to rend his garments. By the Levitical law, this was prohibited under sentence of death. Under no circumstances, on no occasion, was the priest to rend his robe. It was the custom among the Jews for the garments to be rent at the death of friends, but this custom the priests were not to observe. Express command had been given by Christ to Moses concerning this. Lev. 10:6.

Everything worn by the priest was to be whole and without blemish. By those beautiful official garments was represented the character of the great antitype, Jesus Christ. Nothing but perfection, in dress and attitude, in word and spirit, could be acceptable to God. He is holy, and His glory and perfection must be represented by the earthly service. Nothing but perfection could properly represent the sacredness of the heavenly service. Finite man might rend his own heart by showing a contrite and humble spirit. This God would discern. But no rent must be made in the priestly robes, for this would mar the representation of heavenly things. The high priest who dared to appear in holy office, and engage in the service of the sanctuary, with a rent robe, was looked upon as having severed himself from God. By rending his garment he cut himself off from being a representative character. He was no longer accepted by God as an officiating priest. This course of action, as exhibited by Caiaphas, showed human passion, human imperfection.

By rending his garments, Caiaphas made of no effect the law of God, to follow the tradition of men. A man-made law provided that in case of blasphemy a priest might rend his garments in horror at the sin, and be guiltless. Thus the law of God was made void by the laws of men.

Each action of the high priest was watched with interest by the people; and Caiaphas thought for effect to display his piety. But in this act, designed as an accusation against Christ, he was reviling the One of whom God had said, "My name is in Him." Ex. 23:21. He himself was committing blasphemy. Standing under the condemnation of God, he pronounced sentence upon Christ as a blasphemer.

When Caiaphas rent his garment, his act was significant of the place that the Jewish nation as a nation would thereafter occupy toward God. The once favored people of God were separating themselves from Him, and were fast becoming a people disowned by Jehovah. When Christ upon the cross cried out, "It is finished" (John 19:30), and the veil of the temple was rent in twain, the Holy Watcher declared that the Jewish people had rejected Him who was the antitype of all their types, the substance of all their shadows. Israel was divorced from God. Well might Caiaphas then rend his official robes, which signified that he claimed to be a representative of the great High Priest; for no longer had they any meaning for him or for the people. Well might the high priest rend his robes in horror for himself and for the nation.

The Sanhedrin had pronounced Jesus worthy of death; but it was contrary to the Jewish law to try a prisoner by night. In legal condemnation nothing could be done except in the light of day and before a full session of the council. Notwithstanding this, the Saviour was now treated as a condemned criminal, and given up to be abused by the lowest and vilest of humankind. The palace of the high priest surrounded an open court in which the soldiers and the multitude had gathered. Through this court, Jesus was taken to the guardroom, on every side meeting with mockery of His claim to be the Son of God. His own words, "sitting on the right hand of power," and, "coming in the clouds of heaven," were jeeringly repeated. While in the guardroom, awaiting His legal trial, He was not protected. The ignorant rabble had seen the cruelty with which He was treated before the council, and from this they took license to manifest all the satanic elements of their nature. Christ's very nobility and godlike bearing goaded them to madness. His meekness, His innocence, His majestic patience, filled them with hatred born of Satan. Mercy and justice were trampled upon. Never was criminal treated in so inhuman a manner as was the Son of God.

But a keener anguish rent the heart of Jesus; the blow that inflicted the deepest pain no enemy's hand could have dealt. While He was undergoing the mockery of an examination before Caiaphas, Christ had been denied by one of His own disciples.

After deserting their Master in the garden, two of the disciples had ventured to follow, at a distance, the mob that had Jesus in charge. These disciples were Peter and John. The priests recognized John as a well-known disciple of Jesus, and admitted him to the hall, hoping that as he witnessed the humiliation of his Leader, he would scorn the idea of such a one being the Son of God. John spoke in favor of Peter, and gained an entrance for him also.

In the court a fire had been kindled; for it was the coldest hour of the night, being just before the dawn. A company drew about the fire, and Peter presumptuously took his place with them. He did not wish to be recognized as a disciple of Jesus. By mingling carelessly with the crowd, he hoped to be taken for one of those who had brought Jesus to the hall.

But as the light flashed upon Peter's face, the woman who kept the door cast a searching glance upon him. She had noticed that he came in with John, she marked the look of dejection on his face, and thought that he might be a disciple of Jesus. She was one of the servants of Caiaphas' household, and was curious to know. She said to Peter, "Art not thou also one of this Man's disciples?" Peter was startled and confused; the eyes of the company instantly fastened upon him. He pretended not to understand her; but she was persistent, and said to those around her that this man was with Jesus. Peter felt compelled to answer, and said angrily, "Woman, I know Him not." This was the first denial, and immediately the cock crew. O Peter, so soon ashamed of thy Master! so soon to deny thy Lord!

The disciple John, upon entering the judgment hall, did not try to conceal the fact that he was a follower of Jesus. He did not mingle with the rough company who were reviling his Master. He was not questioned, for he did not assume a false character, and thus lay himself liable to suspicion. He sought a retired corner secure from the notice of the mob, but as near Jesus as it was possible for him to be. Here he could see and hear all that took place at the trial of his Lord.

Peter had not designed that his real character should be known. In assuming an air of indifference he had placed himself on the enemy's ground, and he became an easy prey to temptation. If he had been called to fight for his Master, he would have been a courageous soldier; but when the finger of scorn was pointed at him, he proved himself a coward. Many who do not shrink from active warfare for their Lord are driven by ridicule to deny their faith. By associating with those whom they should avoid, they place themselves in the way of temptation. They invite the enemy to tempt them, and are led to say and do that of which under other circumstances they would never have been guilty. The disciple of Christ who in our day disguises his faith through dread of suffering or reproach denies his Lord as really as did Peter in the judgment hall.

Peter tried to show no interest in the trial of his Master, but his heart was wrung with sorrow as he heard the cruel taunts, and saw the abuse He was suffering. More than this, he was surprised and angry that Jesus should humiliate Himself and His followers by submitting to such treatment. In order to conceal his true feelings, he endeavored to join with the persecutors of Jesus in their untimely jests. But his appearance was unnatural. He was acting a lie, and while seeking to talk unconcernedly he could not restrain expressions of indignation at the abuse heaped upon his Master.

Attention was called to him the second time, and he was again charged with being a follower of Jesus. He now declared with an oath, "I do not know the Man." Still another opportunity was given him. An hour had passed, when one of the servants of the high priest, being a near kinsman of the man whose ear Peter had cut off, asked him, "Did not I see thee in the garden with Him?" "Surely thou art one of them: for thou art a Galilean, and thy speech agreeth thereto." At this Peter flew into a rage. The disciples of Jesus were noted for the purity of their language, and in order fully to deceive his questioners, and justify his assumed character, Peter now denied his Master with cursing and swearing. Again the cock crew. Peter heard it then, and he remembered the words of Jesus, "Before the cock crow twice, thou shalt deny Me thrice." Mark 14:30.

While the degrading oaths were fresh upon Peter's lips, and the shrill crowing of the cock was still ringing in his ears, the Saviour turned from the frowning judges, and looked full upon His poor disciple. At the same time Peter's eyes were drawn to his Master. In that gentle countenance he read deep pity and sorrow, but there was no anger there.

The sight of that pale, suffering face, those quivering lips, that look of compassion and forgiveness, pierced his heart like an arrow. Conscience was aroused. Memory was active. Peter called to mind his promise of a few short hours before that he would go with his Lord to prison and to death. He remembered his grief when the Saviour told him in the upper chamber that he would deny his Lord thrice that same night. Peter had just declared that he knew not Jesus, but he now realized with bitter grief how well his Lord knew him, and how accurately He had read his heart, the falseness of which was unknown even to himself.

A tide of memories rushed over him. The Saviour's tender mercy,

His kindness and long-suffering, His gentleness and patience toward His erring disciples,—all was remembered. He recalled the caution, "Simon, behold, Satan hath desired to have you, that he may sift you as wheat: but I have prayed for thee, that thy faith fail not." Luke 22:31, 32. He reflected with horror upon his own ingratitude, his falsehood, his perjury. Once more he looked at his Master, and saw a sacrilegious hand raised to smite Him in the face. Unable longer to endure the scene, he rushed, heartbroken, from the hall.

He pressed on in solitude and darkness, he knew not and cared not whither. At last he found himself in Gethsemane. The scene of a few hours before came vividly to his mind. The suffering face of his Lord, stained with bloody sweat and convulsed with anguish, rose before him. He remembered with bitter remorse that Jesus had wept and agonized in prayer alone, while those who should have united with Him in that trying hour were sleeping. He remembered His solemn charge, "Watch and pray, that ye enter not into temptation." Matt. 26:41. He witnessed again the scene in the judgment hall. It was torture to his bleeding heart to know that he had added the heaviest burden to the Saviour's humiliation and grief. On the very spot where Jesus had poured out His soul in agony to His Father, Peter fell upon his face, and wished that he might die.

It was in sleeping when Jesus bade him watch and pray that Peter had prepared the way for his great sin. All the disciples, by sleeping in that critical hour, sustained a great loss. Christ knew the fiery ordeal through which they were to pass. He knew how Satan would work to paralyze their senses that they might be unready for the trial. Therefore it was that He gave them warning. Had those hours in the garden been spent in watching and prayer, Peter would not have been left to depend upon his own feeble strength. He would not have denied his Lord. Had the disciples watched with Christ in His agony, they would have been prepared to behold His suffering upon the cross. They would have understood in some degree the nature of His overpowering anguish. They would have been able to recall His words that foretold His sufferings, His death, and His resurrection.

Amid the gloom of the most trying hour, some rays of hope would have lighted up the darkness and sustained their faith.

As soon as it was day, the Sanhedrin again assembled, and again Jesus was brought into the council room. He had declared Himself the Son of God, and they had construed His words into a charge against Him. But they could not condemn Him on this, for many of them had not been present at the night session, and they had not heard His words. And they knew that the Roman tribunal would find in them nothing worthy of death. But if from His own lips they could all hear those words repeated, their object might be gained. His claim to the Messiahship they might construe into a seditious political claim.

"Art Thou the Christ?" they said, "tell us." But Christ remained silent. They continued to ply Him with questions. At last in tones of mournful pathos He answered, "If I tell you, ye will not believe; and if I also ask you, ye will not answer Me, nor let Me go." But that they might be left without excuse He added the solemn warning, "Hereafter shall the Son of man sit on the right hand of the power of God."

"Art Thou then the Son of God?" they asked with one voice. He said unto them, "Ye say that I am." They cried out, "What need we any further witness? for we ourselves have heard of His own mouth."

And so by the third condemnation of the Jewish authorities, Jesus was to die. All that was now necessary, they thought, was for the Romans to ratify this condemnation, and deliver Him into their hands.

Then came the third scene of abuse and mockery, worse even than that received from the ignorant rabble. In the very presence of the priests and rulers, and with their sanction, this took place. Every feeling of sympathy or humanity had gone out of their hearts. If their arguments were weak, and failed to silence His voice, they had other weapons, such as in all ages have been used to silence heretics,—suffering, and violence, and death.

When the condemnation of Jesus was pronounced by the judges, a satanic fury took possession of the people. The roar of voices was like that of wild beasts. The crowd made a rush toward Jesus, crying, He is guilty, put Him to death! Had it not been for the Roman soldiers, Jesus would not have lived to be nailed to the cross of Calvary. He would have been torn in pieces before His judges, had not Roman authority interfered, and by force of arms restrained the violence of the mob.

Heathen men were angry at the brutal treatment of one against whom nothing had been proved. The Roman officers declared that the Jews in pronouncing condemnation upon Jesus were infringing upon the Roman power, and that it was even against the Jewish law to condemn a man to death upon his own testimony. This intervention brought a momentary lull in the proceedings; but the Jewish leaders were dead alike to pity and to shame.

Priests and rulers forgot the dignity of their office, and abused the Son of God with foul epithets. They taunted Him with His parentage. They declared that His presumption in proclaiming Himself the Messiah made Him deserving of the most ignominious death. The most dissolute men engaged in infamous abuse of the Saviour. An old garment was thrown over His head, and His persecutors struck Him in the face, saying, "Prophesy unto us, Thou Christ, Who is he that smote Thee?" When the garment was removed, one poor wretch spat in His face.

The angels of God faithfully recorded every insulting look, word, and act against their beloved Commander. One day the base men who scorned and spat upon the calm, pale face of Christ will look upon it in its glory, shining brighter than the sun.

THREE

JUDAS

The history of Judas presents the sad ending of a life that might have been honored of God. Had Judas died before his last journey to Jerusalem he would have been regarded as a man worthy of a place among the twelve, and one who would be greatly missed. The abhorrence which has followed him through the centuries would not have existed but for the attributes revealed at the close of his history. But it was for a purpose that his character was laid open to the world. It was to be a warning to all who, like him, should betray sacred trusts.

A little before the Passover, Judas had renewed his contract with the priests to deliver Jesus into their hands. Then it was arranged that the Saviour should be taken at one of His resorts for meditation and prayer. Since the feast at the house of Simon, Judas had had opportunity to reflect upon the deed which he had covenanted to perform, but his purpose was unchanged. For thirty pieces of silver—the price of a slave—he sold the Lord of glory to ignominy and death.

Judas had naturally a strong love for money; but he had not always been corrupt enough to do such a deed as this. He had fostered the evil spirit of avarice until it had become the ruling motive of his life. The love of mammon overbalanced his love for Christ. Through becoming the slave of one vice he gave himself to Satan, to be driven to any lengths in sin.

Judas had joined the disciples when multitudes were following Christ. The Saviour's teaching moved their hearts as they hung entranced upon His words, spoken in the synagogue, by the seaside, upon the mount. Judas saw the sick, the lame, the blind, flock to Jesus from the towns and cities. He saw the dying laid at His feet. He witnessed the Saviour's mighty works in healing the sick, casting out devils, and raising the dead. He felt in his own person the evidence of Christ's power. He recognized the teaching of Christ as superior to all that he had ever heard. He loved the Great Teacher, and desired to be with Him. He felt a desire to be changed in character and life, and he hoped to experience this through connecting himself with Jesus. The Saviour did not repulse Judas. He gave him a place among the twelve. He trusted him to do the work of an evangelist. He endowed him with power to heal the sick and to cast out devils. But Judas did not come to the point of surrendering himself fully to Christ. He did not give up his worldly ambition or his love of money. While he accepted the position of a minister of Christ, he did not bring himself under the divine molding. He felt that he could retain his own judgment and opinions, and he cultivated a disposition to criticize and accuse.

Judas was highly regarded by the disciples, and had great influence over them. He himself had a high opinion of his own qualifications, and looked upon his brethren as greatly inferior to him in judgment and ability. They did not see their opportunities, he thought, and take advantage of circumstances. The church would never prosper with such shortsighted men as leaders. Peter was impetuous; he would move without consideration. John, who was treasuring up the truths that fell from Christ's lips, was looked upon by Judas as a poor financier. Matthew, whose training had taught him accuracy in all things, was very particular in regard to honesty, and he was ever contemplating the words of Christ, and became so absorbed in them that, as Judas thought, he could not be trusted to do sharp, far-seeing business. Thus Judas summed up all the disciples, and flattered himself that the church would often be brought into perplexity and embarrassment if it were not for his ability as a manager. Judas regarded himself as the capable one, who could not be overreached. In his own estimation he was an honor to the cause, and as such he always represented himself.

Judas was blinded to his own weakness of character, and Christ placed him where he would have an opportunity to see and correct this. As treasurer for the disciples, he was called upon to provide for the needs of the little company, and to relieve the necessities of the poor. When in the Passover chamber Jesus said to him, "That thou doest, do quickly" (John 13:27), the disciples thought He had bidden him buy what was needed for the feast, or give something to the poor. In ministering to others, Judas might have developed an unselfish spirit. But while listening daily to the lessons of Christ and witnessing His unselfish life, Judas indulged his covetous disposition. The small sums that came into his hands were a continual temptation. Often when he did a little service for Christ, or devoted time to religious purposes, he paid himself out of this meager fund. In his own eyes these pretexts served to excuse his action; but in God's sight he was a thief.

Christ's oft-repeated statement that His kingdom was not of this world offended Judas. He had marked out a line upon which he expected Christ to work. He had planned that John the Baptist should be delivered from prison. But lo, John was left to be beheaded. And Jesus, instead of asserting His royal right and avenging the death of John, retired with His disciples into a country place. Judas wanted more aggressive warfare. He thought that if Jesus would not prevent the disciples from carrying out their schemes, the work would be more successful. He marked the increasing enmity of the Jewish leaders, and saw their challenge unheeded when they demanded from Christ a sign from heaven. His heart was open to unbelief, and the enemy supplied thoughts of questioning and rebellion. Why did Jesus dwell so much upon that which was discouraging? Why did He predict trial and persecution for Himself and for His disciples? The prospect of having a high place in the new kingdom had led Judas to espouse the cause of Christ. Were his hopes to be disappointed? Judas had not decided that Jesus was not the Son of God; but he was questioning, and seeking to find some explanation of His mighty works.

Notwithstanding the Saviour's own teaching, Judas was continually advancing the idea that Christ would reign as king in Jerusalem. At the feeding of the five thousand he tried to bring this about. On this occasion Judas assisted in distributing the food to the hungry multitude. He had an opportunity to see the benefit which it was in his power to impart to others. He felt the satisfaction that always comes in service to God. He helped to bring the sick and suffering from among the multitude to Christ. He saw what relief, what joy and gladness, come to human hearts through the healing power of the Restorer. He might have comprehended the methods of Christ. But he was blinded by his own selfish desires. Judas was first to take advantage of the enthusiasm excited by the miracle of the loaves. It was he who set on foot the project to take Christ by force and make Him king. His hopes were high. His disappointment was bitter.

Christ's discourse in the synagogue concerning the bread of life was the turning point in the history of Judas. He heard the words, "Except ye eat the flesh of the Son of man, and drink His blood, ye have no life in you." John 6:53. He saw that Christ was offering spiritual rather than worldly good. He regarded himself as farsighted, and thought he could see that Jesus would have no honor, and that He could bestow no high position upon His followers. He determined not to unite himself so closely to Christ but that he could draw away. He would watch. And he did watch.

From that time he expressed doubts that confused the disciples. He introduced controversies and misleading sentiments, repeating the arguments urged by the scribes and Pharisees against the claims of Christ. All the little and large troubles and crosses, the difficulties and the apparent hindrances to the advancement of the gospel, Judas interpreted as evidences against its truthfulness. He would introduce texts of Scripture that had no connection with the truths Christ was presenting. These texts, separated from their connection, perplexed the disciples, and increased the discouragement that was constantly pressing upon them. Yet all this was done by Judas in such a way as to make it appear that he was conscientious. And while the disciples were searching for evidence to confirm the words of the Great Teacher, Judas would lead them almost imperceptibly on another track. Thus in a very religious, and apparently wise, way he was presenting matters in a different light from that in which Jesus had given them, and attaching to His words a meaning that He had not conveyed. His suggestions were constantly exciting an ambitious desire for temporal preferment, and thus turning the disciples from the important things they should have considered. The dissension as to which of them should be greatest was generally excited by Judas.

When Jesus presented to the rich young ruler the condition of discipleship, Judas was displeased. He thought that a mistake had been made. If such men as this ruler could be connected with the believers, they would help sustain Christ's cause. If Judas were only received as a counselor, he thought, he could suggest many plans for the advantage of the little church. His principles and methods would differ somewhat from Christ's, but in these things he thought himself wiser than Christ.

In all that Christ said to His disciples, there was something with which, in heart, Judas disagreed. Under his influence the leaven of disaffection was fast doing its work. The disciples did not see the real agency in all this; but Jesus saw that Satan was communicating his attributes to Judas, and thus opening up a channel through which to influence the other disciples. This, a year before the betrayal, Christ declared. "Have not I chosen you twelve," He said, "and one of you is a devil?" John 6:70.

Yet Judas made no open opposition, nor seemed to question the Saviour's lessons. He made no outward murmur until the time of the feast in Simon's house. When Mary anointed the Saviour's feet, Judas manifested his covetous disposition. At the reproof from Jesus his very spirit seemed turned to gall. Wounded pride and desire for revenge broke down the barriers, and the greed so long indulged held him in control. This will be the experience of everyone who persists in tampering with sin. The elements of depravity that are not resisted and overcome, respond to Satan's temptation, and the soul is led captive at his will.

But Judas was not yet wholly hardened. Even after he had twice pledged himself to betray the Saviour, there was opportunity for repentance. At the Passover supper Jesus proved His divinity by revealing the traitor's purpose. He tenderly included Judas in the ministry to the disciples. But the last appeal of love was unheeded. Then the case of Judas was decided, and the feet that Jesus had washed went forth to the betrayer's work.

Judas reasoned that if Jesus was to be crucified, the event must come to pass. His own act in betraying the Saviour would not change the result. If Jesus was not to die, it would only force Him to deliver Himself. At all events, Judas would gain something by his treachery. He counted that he had made a sharp bargain in betraying his Lord.

Judas did not, however, believe that Christ would permit Himself to be arrested. In betraying Him, it was his purpose to teach Him a lesson. He intended to play a part that would make the Saviour careful thenceforth to treat him with due respect. But Judas knew not that he was giving Christ up to death. How often, as the Saviour taught in parables, the scribes and Pharisees had been carried away with His striking illustrations! How often they had pronounced judgment against themselves! Often when the truth was brought home to their hearts, they had been filled with rage, and had taken up stones to cast at Him; but again and again He had made His escape. Since He had escaped so many snares, thought Judas, He certainly would not now allow Himself to be taken.

Judas decided to put the matter to the test. If Jesus really was the Messiah, the people, for whom He had done so much, would rally about Him, and would proclaim Him king. This would forever settle many minds that were now in uncertainty. Judas would have the credit of having placed the king on David's throne. And this act would secure to him the first position, next to Christ, in the new kingdom

The false disciple acted his part in betraying Jesus. In the garden, when he said to the leaders of the mob, "Whomsoever I shall kiss, that same is He: hold Him fast" (Matt. 26:48), he fully believed that Christ would escape out of their hands. Then if they should blame him, he could say, Did I not tell you to hold Him fast?

Judas beheld the captors of Christ, acting upon his words, bind Him firmly. In amazement he saw that the Saviour suffered Himself to be led away. Anxiously he followed Him from the garden to the trial before the Jewish rulers. At every movement he looked for Him to surprise His enemies, by appearing before them as the Son of God, and setting at nought all their plots and power. But as hour after hour went by, and Jesus submitted to all the abuse heaped upon Him, a terrible fear came to the traitor that he had sold his Master to His death.

As the trial drew to a close, Judas could endure the torture of his guilty conscience no longer. Suddenly a hoarse voice rang through the hall, sending a thrill of terror to all hearts: He is innocent; spare Him, O Caiaphas!

The tall form of Judas was now seen pressing through the startled throng. His face was pale and haggard, and great drops of sweat stood on his forehead. Rushing to the throne of judgment, he threw down before the high priest the pieces of silver that had been the price of his Lord's betrayal. Eagerly grasping the robe of Caiaphas, he implored him to release Jesus, declaring that He had done nothing worthy of death. Caiaphas angrily shook him off, but was confused, and knew not what to say. The perfidy of the priests was revealed. It was evident that they had bribed the disciple to betray his Master.

"I have sinned," again cried Judas, "in that I have betrayed the innocent blood." But the high priest, regaining his self-possession, answered with scorn, "What is that to us? see thou to that." Matt. 27:4. The priests had been willing to make Judas their tool; but they despised his baseness. When he turned to them with confession, they spurned him.

Judas now cast himself at the feet of Jesus, acknowledging Him to be the Son of God, and entreating Him to deliver Himself. The Saviour did not reproach His betrayer. He knew that Judas did not repent; his confession was forced from his guilty soul by an awful sense of condemnation and a looking for of judgment, but he felt no deep, heartbreaking grief that he had betrayed the spotless Son of God, and denied the Holy One of Israel. Yet Jesus spoke no word of condemnation. He looked pityingly upon Judas, and said, For this hour came I into the world.

A murmur of surprise ran through the assembly. With amazement they beheld the forbearance of Christ toward His betrayer. Again there swept over them the conviction that this Man was more than mortal. But if He was the Son of God, they questioned, why did He not free Himself from His bonds and triumph over His accusers?

Judas saw that his entreaties were in vain, and he rushed from the hall exclaiming, It is too late! It is too late! He felt that he could not live to see Jesus crucified, and in despair went out and hanged himself.

Later that same day, on the road from Pilate's hall to Calvary, there came an interruption to the shouts and jeers of the wicked throng who were leading Jesus to the place of crucifixion. As they passed a retired spot, they saw at the foot of a lifeless tree, the body of Judas. It was a most revolting sight. His weight had broken the cord by which he had hanged himself to the tree. In falling, his body had been horribly mangled, and dogs were now devouring it. His remains were immediately buried out of sight; but there was less mockery among the throng, and many a pale face revealed the thoughts within. Retribution seemed already visiting those who were guilty of the blood of Jesus.

FOUR

IN PILATE'S JUDGMENT HALL

I n the judgment hall of Pilate, the Roman governor, Christ stands bound as a prisoner. About Him are the guard of soldiers, and the hall is fast filling with spectators. Just outside the entrance are the judges of the Sanhedrin, priests, rulers, elders, and the mob.

After condemning Jesus, the council of the Sanhedrin had come to Pilate to have the sentence confirmed and executed. But these Jewish officials would not enter the Roman judgment hall. According to their ceremonial law they would be defiled thereby, and thus prevented from taking part in the feast of the Passover. In their blindness they did not see that murderous hatred had defiled their hearts. They did not see that Christ was the real Passover lamb, and that, since they had rejected Him, the great feast had for them lost its significance.

When the Saviour was brought into the judgment hall, Pilate looked upon Him with no friendly eyes. The Roman governor had been called from his bedchamber in haste, and he determined to do his work as quickly as possible. He was prepared to deal with the prisoner with magisterial severity. Assuming his severest expression, he turned to see what kind of man he had to examine, that he had been called from his repose at so early an hour. He knew that it must be someone whom the Jewish authorities were anxious to have tried and punished with haste.

Pilate looked at the men who had Jesus in charge, and then his gaze rested searchingly on Jesus. He had had to deal with all kinds of criminals; but never before had a man bearing marks of such goodness and nobility been brought before him. On His face he saw no sign of guilt, no expression of fear, no boldness or defiance. He saw a man of calm and dignified bearing, whose countenance bore not the marks of a criminal, but the signature of heaven.

Christ's appearance made a favorable impression upon Pilate. His better nature was roused. He had heard of Jesus and His works. His wife had told him something of the wonderful deeds performed by the Galilean prophet, who cured the sick and raised the dead. Now this revived as a dream in Pilate's mind. He recalled rumors that he had heard from several sources. He resolved to demand of the Jews their charges against the prisoner.

Who is this Man, and wherefore have ye brought Him? he said. What accusation bring ye against Him? The Jews were disconcerted. Knowing that they could not substantiate their charges against Christ, they did not desire a public examination. They answered that He was a deceiver called Jesus of Nazareth.

Again Pilate asked, "What accusation bring ye against this Man?" The priests did not answer his question, but in words that showed their irritation, they said, "If He were not a malefactor, we would not have delivered Him up unto thee." When those composing the Sanhedrin, the first men of the nation, bring to you a man they deem worthy of death, is there need to ask for an accusation against him? They hoped to impress Pilate with a sense of their importance, and thus lead him to accede to their request without going through many preliminaries. They were eager to have their sentence ratified; for they knew that the people who had witnessed Christ's marvelous works could tell a story very different from the fabrication they themselves were now rehearsing.

The priests thought that with the weak and vacillating Pilate they could carry through their plans without trouble. Before this he had signed the death warrant hastily, condemning to death men they knew were not worthy of death. In his estimation the life of a prisoner was of little account; whether he were innocent or guilty was of no special consequence. The priests hoped that Pilate would now inflict the death penalty on Jesus without giving Him a hearing. This they besought as a favor on the occasion of their great national festival.

But there was something in the prisoner that held Pilate back from this. He dared not do it. He read the purposes of the priests. He remembered how, not long before, Jesus had raised Lazarus, a man that had been dead four days; and he determined to know, before signing the sentence of condemnation, what were the charges against Him, and whether they could be proved.

If your judgment is sufficient, he said, why bring the prisoner to me? "Take ye Him, and judge Him according to your law." Thus pressed, the priests said that they had already passed sentence upon Him, but that they must have Pilate's sentence to render their condemnation valid. What is your sentence? Pilate asked. The death sentence, they answered; but it is not lawful for us to put any man to death. They asked Pilate to take their word as to Christ's guilt, and enforce their sentence. They would take the responsibility of the result.

Pilate was not a just or a conscientious judge; but weak though he was in moral power, he refused to grant this request. He would not condemn Jesus until a charge had been brought against Him.

The priests were in a dilemma. They saw that they must cloak their hypocrisy under the thickest concealment. They must not allow it to appear that Christ had been arrested on religious grounds. Were this put forward as a reason, their proceedings would have no weight with Pilate. They must make it appear that Jesus was working against the common law; then He could be punished as a political offender. Tumults and insurrection against the Roman government were constantly arising among the Jews. With these revolts the Romans had dealt very rigorously, and they were constantly on the watch to repress everything that could lead to an outbreak.

Only a few days before this the Pharisees had tried to entrap Christ with the question, "Is it lawful for us to give tribute unto Caesar?" But Christ had unveiled their hypocrisy. The Romans who were present had seen the utter failure of the plotters, and their discomfiture at His answer, "Render therefore unto Caesar the things which be Caesar's." Luke 20:22-25.

Now the priests thought to make it appear that on this occasion Christ had taught what they hoped He would teach. In their extremity they called false witnesses to their aid, "and they began to accuse Him, saying, We found this fellow perverting the nation, and forbidding to give tribute to Caesar, saying that He Himself is Christ a King." Three charges, each without foundation. The priests knew this, but they were willing to commit perjury could they but secure their end.

Pilate saw through their purpose. He did not believe that the prisoner had plotted against the government. His meek and humble appearance was altogether out of harmony with the charge. Pilate was convinced that a deep plot had been laid to destroy an innocent man who stood in the way of the Jewish dignitaries. Turning to Jesus he asked, "Art Thou the King of the Jews?" The Saviour answered, "Thou sayest it." And as He spoke, His countenance lighted up as if a sunbeam were shining upon it.

When they heard His answer, Caiaphas and those that were with him called Pilate to witness that Jesus had admitted the crime with which He was charged. With noisy cries, priests, scribes, and rulers demanded that He be sentenced to death. The cries were taken up by the mob, and the uproar was deafening. Pilate was confused. Seeing that Jesus made no answer to His accusers, Pilate said to Him, "Answerest Thou nothing? behold how many things they witness against Thee. But Jesus yet answered nothing."

Standing behind Pilate, in view of all in the court, Christ heard the abuse; but to all the false charges against Him He answered not a word. His whole bearing gave evidence of conscious innocence. He stood unmoved by the fury of the waves that beat about Him. It was as if the heavy surges of wrath, rising higher and higher, like the waves of the boisterous ocean, broke about Him, but did not touch Him. He stood silent, but His silence was eloquence. It was as a light shining from the inner to the outer man.

Pilate was astonished at His bearing. Does this Man disregard the proceedings because He does not care to save His life? he asked himself. As he looked at Jesus, bearing insult and mockery without retaliation, he felt that He could not be as unrighteous and unjust as were the clamoring priests. Hoping to gain the truth from Him and to escape the tumult of the crowd, Pilate took Jesus aside with him, and again questioned, "Art Thou the King of the Jews?"

Jesus did not directly answer this question. He knew that the Holy Spirit was striving with Pilate, and He gave him opportunity to acknowledge his conviction. "Sayest thou this thing of thyself," He asked, "or did others tell it thee of Me?" That is, was it the accusations of the priests, or a desire to receive light from Christ, that prompted Pilate's question? Pilate understood Christ's meaning; but pride arose in his heart. He would not acknowledge the conviction that pressed upon him. "Am I a Jew?" he said. "Thine own nation and the chief priests have delivered Thee unto me: what hast Thou done?"

Pilate's golden opportunity had passed. Yet Jesus did not leave him without further light. While He did not directly answer Pilate's question, He plainly stated His own mission. He gave Pilate to understand that He was not seeking an earthly throne.

"My kingdom is not of this world," He said; "if My kingdom were of this world, then would My servants fight, that I should not be delivered to the Jews: but now is My kingdom not from hence. Pilate therefore said unto Him, Art Thou a king then? Jesus answered, Thou sayest that I am a king. To this end was I born, and for this cause came I into the world, that I should bear witness unto the truth. Everyone that is of the truth heareth My voice."

Christ affirmed that His word was in itself a key which would unlock the mystery to those who were prepared to receive it. It had a self-commending power, and this was the secret of the spread of His kingdom of truth. He desired Pilate to understand that only by receiving and appropriating truth could his ruined nature be reconstructed.

Pilate had a desire to know the truth. His mind was confused. He eagerly grasped the words of the Saviour, and his heart was stirred with a great longing to know what it really was, and how he could obtain it. "What is truth?" he inquired. But he did not wait for an answer. The tumult outside recalled him to the interests of the hour; for the priests were clamorous for immediate action. Going out to the Jews, he declared emphatically, "I find in Him no fault at all."

These words from a heathen judge were a scathing rebuke to the perfidy and falsehood of the rulers of Israel who were accusing the Saviour. As the priests and elders heard this from Pilate, their disappointment and rage knew no bounds. They had long plotted and waited for this opportunity. As they saw the prospect of the release of Jesus, they seemed ready to tear Him in pieces. They loudly denounced Pilate, and threatened him with the censure of the Roman government. They accused him of refusing to condemn Jesus, who, they affirmed, had set Himself up against Caesar.

Angry voices were now heard, declaring that the seditious influence of Jesus was well known throughout the country. The priests said, "He stirreth up the people, teaching throughout all Jewry, beginning from Galilee to this place."

Pilate at this time had no thought of condemning Jesus. He knew that the Jews had accused Him through hatred and prejudice. He knew what his duty was. Justice demanded that Christ should be immediately released. But Pilate dreaded the ill will of the people. Should he refuse to give Jesus into their hands, a tumult would be raised, and this he feared to meet. When he heard that Christ was from Galilee, he decided to send Him to Herod, the ruler of that province, who was then in Jerusalem. By this course, Pilate thought to shift the responsibility of the trial from himself to Herod. He also thought this a good opportunity to heal an old quarrel between himself and Herod. And so it proved. The two magistrates made friends over the trial of the Saviour.

Pilate delivered Jesus again to the soldiers, and amid the jeers and insults of the mob He was hurried to the judgment hall of Herod. "When Herod saw Jesus, he was exceeding glad." He had never before met the Saviour, but "he was desirous to see Him of a long season, because he had heard many things of Him; and he hoped to have seen some miracle done by Him." This Herod was he whose hands were stained with the blood of John the Baptist. When Herod first heard of Jesus, he was terror-stricken, and said, "It is John, whom I beheaded: he is risen from the dead;" "therefore mighty works do show forth themselves in him." Mark 6:16; Matt. 14:2. Yet Herod desired to see Jesus. Now there was opportunity to save the life of this prophet, and the king hoped to banish forever from his mind the memory of that bloody head brought to him in a charger. He also desired to have his curiosity gratified, and thought that if Christ were given any prospect of release, He would do anything that was asked of Him.

A large company of the priests and elders had accompanied Christ to Herod. And when the Saviour was brought in, these dignitaries, all speaking excitedly, urged their accusations against Him. But Herod paid little regard to their charges. He commanded silence, desiring an opportunity to question Christ. He ordered that the fetters of Christ should be unloosed, at the same time charging His enemies with roughly treating Him. Looking with compassion into the serene face of the world's Redeemer, he read in it only wisdom and purity. He as well as Pilate was satisfied that Christ had been accused through malice and envy.

Herod questioned Christ in many words, but throughout the Saviour maintained a profound silence. At the command of the king, the decrepit and maimed were then called in, and Christ was ordered to prove His claims by working a miracle. Men say that Thou canst heal the sick, said Herod. I am anxious to see that Thy widespread fame has not been belied. Jesus did not respond, and Herod still continued to urge: If Thou canst work miracles for others, work them now for Thine own good, and it will serve Thee a good purpose. Again he commanded, Show us a sign that Thou hast the power with which rumor hath accredited Thee. But Christ was as one who heard and saw not. The Son of God had taken upon Himself man's nature. He must do as man must do in like circumstances. Therefore He would not work a miracle to save Himself the pain and humiliation that man must endure when placed in a similar position.

Herod promised that if Christ would perform some miracle in his presence, He should be released. Christ's accusers had seen with their own eyes the mighty works wrought by His power. They had heard Him command the grave to give up its dead. They had seen the dead come forth obedient to His voice. Fear seized them lest He should now work a miracle. Of all things they most dreaded an exhibition of His power. Such a manifestation would prove a deathblow to their plans, and would perhaps cost them their lives. Again the priests and rulers, in great anxiety, urged their accusations against Him. Raising their voices, they declared, He is a traitor, a blasphemer. He works His miracles through the power given Him by Beelzebub, the prince of the devils. The hall became a scene of confusion, some crying one thing and some another.

Herod's conscience was now far less sensitive than when he had trembled with horror at the request of Herodias for the head of John the Baptist. For a time he had felt the keen stings of remorse for his terrible act; but his moral perceptions had become more and more degraded by his licentious life. Now his heart had become so hardened that he could even boast of the punishment he had inflicted upon John for daring to reprove him. And he now threatened Jesus, declaring repeatedly that he had power to release or to condemn Him. But no sign from Jesus gave evidence that He heard a word.

Herod was irritated by this silence. It seemed to indicate utter indifference to his authority. To the vain and pompous king, open rebuke would have been less offensive than to be thus ignored. Again he angrily threatened Jesus, who still remained unmoved and silent.

The mission of Christ in this world was not to gratify idle curiosity. He came to heal the brokenhearted. Could He have spoken any word to heal the bruises of sin-sick souls, He would not have kept silent. But He had no words for those who would but trample the truth under their unholy feet.

Christ might have spoken words to Herod that would have pierced the ears of the hardened king. He might have stricken him with fear and trembling by laying before him the full iniquity of his life, and the horror of his approaching doom. But Christ's silence was the severest rebuke that He could have given. Herod had rejected the truth spoken to him by the greatest of the prophets, and no other message was he to receive. Not a word had the Majesty of heaven for him. That ear that had ever been open to human woe, had no room for Herod's commands. Those eyes that had ever rested upon the penitent sinner in pitying, forgiving love had no look to bestow upon Herod. Those lips that had uttered the most impressive truth, that in tones of tenderest entreaty had pleaded with the most sinful and the most degraded, were closed to the haughty king who felt no need of a Saviour.

Herod's face grew dark with passion. Turning to the multitude, he angrily denounced Jesus as an impostor. Then to Christ he said, If You will give no evidence of Your claim, I will deliver You up to the soldiers and the people. They may succeed in making You speak. If You are an impostor, death at their hands is only what You merit; if You are the Son of God, save Yourself by working a miracle.

No sooner were these words spoken than a rush was made for Christ. Like wild beasts, the crowd darted upon their prey. Jesus was dragged this way and that, Herod joining the mob in seeking to humiliate the Son of God. Had not the Roman soldiers interposed, and forced back the maddened throng, the Saviour would have been torn in pieces.

"Herod with his men of war set Him at nought, and mocked Him, and arrayed Him in a gorgeous robe." The Roman soldiers joined in this abuse. All that these wicked, corrupt soldiers, helped on by Herod and the Jewish dignitaries, could instigate was heaped upon the Saviour. Yet His divine patience failed not.

Christ's persecutors had tried to measure His character by their own; they had represented Him as vile as themselves. But back of all the present appearance another scene intruded itself,—a scene which they will one day see in all its glory. There were some who trembled in Christ's presence. While the rude throng were bowing in mockery before Him, some who came forward for that purpose turned back, afraid and silenced. Herod was convicted. The last rays of merciful light were shining upon his sin-hardened heart. He felt that this was no common man; for divinity had flashed through humanity. At the very time when Christ was encompassed by mockers, adulterers, and murderers, Herod felt that he was beholding a God upon His throne.

Hardened as he was, Herod dared not ratify the condemnation of Christ. He wished to relieve himself of the terrible responsibility, and he sent Jesus back to the Roman judgment hall.

Pilate was disappointed and much displeased. When the Jews returned with their prisoner, he asked impatiently what they would have him do. He reminded them that he had already examined Jesus, and found no fault in Him; he told them that they had brought complaints against Him, but they had not been able to prove a single charge. He had sent Jesus to Herod, the tetrarch of Galilee, and one of their own nation, but he also had found in Him nothing worthy of death. "I will therefore chastise Him," Pilate said, "and release Him."

Here Pilate showed his weakness. He had declared that Jesus was innocent, yet he was willing for Him to be scourged to pacify His accusers. He would sacrifice justice and principle in order to compromise with the mob. This placed him at a disadvantage. The crowd presumed upon his indecision, and clamored the more for the life of the prisoner. If at the first Pilate had stood firm, refusing to condemn a man whom he found guiltless, he would have broken the fatal chain that was to bind him in remorse and guilt as long as he lived. Had he carried out his convictions of right, the Jews would not have presumed to dictate to him. Christ would have been put to death, but the guilt would not have rested upon Pilate. But Pilate had taken step after step in the violation of his conscience. He had excused himself from judging with justice and equity, and he now found himself almost helpless in the hands of the priests and rulers. His wavering and indecision proved his ruin.

Even now Pilate was not left to act blindly. A message from God warned him from the deed he was about to commit. In answer to Christ's prayer, the wife of Pilate had been visited by an angel from heaven, and in a dream she had beheld the Saviour and conversed with Him. Pilate's wife was not a Jew, but as she looked upon Jesus in her dream, she had no doubt of His character or mission. She knew Him to be the Prince of God. She saw Him on trial in the judgment hall. She saw the hands tightly bound as the hands of a criminal. She saw Herod and his soldiers doing their dreadful work. She heard the priests and rulers, filled with envy and malice, madly accusing. She heard the words, "We have a law, and by our law He ought to die." She saw Pilate give Jesus to the scourging, after he had declared, "I find no fault in Him." She heard the condemnation pronounced by Pilate, and saw him give Christ up to His murderers. She saw the cross uplifted on Calvary. She saw the earth wrapped in darkness, and heard the mysterious cry, "It is finished." Still another scene met her gaze. She saw Christ seated upon the great white cloud, while the earth reeled in space, and His murderers fled from the presence of His glory. With a cry of horror she awoke, and at once wrote to Pilate words of warning.

While Pilate was hesitating as to what he should do, a messenger pressed through the crowd, and handed him the letter from his wife, which read:

"Have thou nothing to do with that just Man: for I have suffered many things this day in a dream because of Him."

Pilate's face grew pale. He was confused by his own conflicting emotions. But while he had been delaying to act, the priests and rulers were still further inflaming the minds of the people. Pilate was forced to action. He now bethought himself of a custom which might serve to secure Christ's release. It was customary at this feast to release some one prisoner whom the people might choose. This custom was of pagan invention; there was not a shadow of justice in it, but it was greatly prized by the Jews. The Roman authorities at this time held a prisoner named Barabbas, who was under sentence of death. This man had claimed to be the Messiah. He claimed authority to establish a different order of things, to set the world right. Under satanic delusion he claimed that whatever he could obtain by theft and robbery was his own. He had done wonderful things through satanic agencies, he had gained a following among the people, and had excited sedition against the Roman government. Under cover of religious enthusiasm he was a hardened and desperate villain, bent on rebellion and cruelty. By giving the people a choice between this man and the innocent Saviour, Pilate thought to arouse them to a sense of justice. He hoped to gain their sympathy for Jesus in opposition to the priests and rulers. So, turning to the crowd, he said with great earnestness, "Whom will ye that I release unto you? Barabbas, or Jesus which is called Christ?"

Like the bellowing of wild beasts came the answer of the mob, "Release unto us Barabbas!" Louder and louder swelled the cry, Barabbas! Barabbas! Thinking that the people had not understood his question, Pilate asked, "Will ye that I release unto you the King of the Jews?" But they cried out again, "Away with this Man, and release unto us Barabbas"! "What shall I do then with Jesus which is called Christ?" Pilate asked. Again the surging multitude roared like demons. Demons themselves, in human form, were in the crowd, and what could be expected but the answer, "Let Him be crucified"?

Pilate was troubled. He had not thought it would come to that. He shrank from delivering an innocent man to the most ignominious and cruel death that could be inflicted. After the roar of voices had ceased, he turned to the people, saying, "Why, what evil hath He done?" But the case had gone too far for argument. It was not evidence of Christ's innocence that they wanted, but His condemnation.

Still Pilate endeavored to save Him. "He said unto them the third time, Why, what evil hath He done? I have found no cause of death in Him: I will therefore chastise Him, and let Him go." But the very mention of His release stirred the people to a tenfold frenzy. "Crucify Him, crucify Him," they cried. Louder and louder swelled the storm that Pilate's indecision had called forth.

Jesus was taken, faint with weariness and covered with wounds, and scourged in the sight of the multitude. "And the soldiers led Him away into the hall, called Praetorium, and they call together the whole band. And they clothed Him with purple, and platted a crown of thorns, and put it about His head, and began to salute Him, Hail, King of the Jews! And they . . . did spit upon Him, and bowing their knees worshiped Him." Occasionally some wicked hand snatched the reed that had been placed in His hand, and struck the crown upon His brow, forcing the thorns into His temples, and sending the blood trickling down His face and beard.

Wonder, O heavens! and be astonished, O earth! Behold the oppressor and the oppressed. A maddened throng enclose the Saviour of the world. Mocking and jeering are mingled with the coarse oaths of blasphemy. His lowly birth and humble life are commented upon by the unfeeling mob. His claim to be the Son of God is ridiculed, and the vulgar jest and insulting sneer are passed from lip to lip.

Satan led the cruel mob in its abuse of the Saviour. It was his purpose to provoke Him to retaliation if possible, or to drive Him to perform a miracle to release Himself, and thus break up the plan of salvation. One stain upon His human life, one failure of His humanity to endure the terrible test, and the Lamb of God would have been an imperfect offering, and the redemption of man a failure. But He who by a command could bring the heavenly host to His aid—He who could have driven that mob in terror from His sight by the flashing forth of His divine majesty—submitted with perfect calmness to the coarsest insult and outrage.

Christ's enemies had demanded a miracle as evidence of His divinity. They had evidence far greater than any they had sought. As their cruelty degraded His torturers below humanity into the likeness of Satan, so did His meekness and patience exalt Jesus above humanity, and prove His kinship to God. His abasement was the pledge of His exaltation. The blood drops of agony that from His wounded temples flowed down His face and beard were the pledge of His anointing with "the oil of gladness" (Heb. 1:9.) as our great high priest.

Satan's rage was great as he saw that all the abuse inflicted upon the Saviour had not forced the least murmur from His lips. Although He had taken upon Him the nature of man, He was sustained by a godlike fortitude, and departed in no particular from the will of His Father.

When Pilate gave Jesus up to be scourged and mocked, he thought to excite the pity of the multitude. He hoped they would decide that this was sufficient punishment. Even the malice of the priests, he thought, would now be satisfied. But with keen perception the Jews saw the weakness of thus punishing a man who had been declared innocent. They knew that Pilate was trying to save the life of the prisoner, and they were determined that Jesus should not be released. To please and satisfy us, Pilate has scourged Him, they thought, and if we press the matter to a decided issue, we shall surely gain our end.

Pilate now sent for Barabbas to be brought into the court. He then presented the two prisoners side by side, and pointing to the Saviour he said in a voice of solemn entreaty, "Behold the Man!" "I bring Him forth to you, that ye may know that I find no fault in Him."

There stood the Son of God, wearing the robe of mockery and the crown of thorns. Stripped to the waist, His back showed the long, cruel stripes, from which the blood flowed freely. His face was stained with blood, and bore the marks of exhaustion and pain; but never had it appeared more beautiful than now. The Saviour's visage was not marred before His enemies. Every feature expressed gentleness and resignation and the tenderest pity for His cruel foes. In His manner there was no cowardly weakness, but the strength and dignity of long-suffering. In striking contrast was the prisoner at His side. Every line of the countenance of Barabbas proclaimed him the hardened ruffian that he was. The contrast spoke to every beholder. Some of the spectators were weeping. As they looked upon Jesus, their hearts were full of sympathy. Even the priests and rulers were convicted that He was all that He claimed to be.

The Roman soldiers that surrounded Christ were not all hardened; some were looking earnestly into His face for one evidence that He was a criminal or dangerous character. From time to time they would turn and cast a look of contempt upon Barabbas. It needed no deep insight to read him through and through. Again they would turn to the One upon trial. They looked at the divine sufferer with feelings of deep pity. The silent submission of Christ stamped upon their minds the scene, never to be effaced until they either acknowledged Him as the Christ, or by rejecting Him decided their own destiny.

Pilate was filled with amazement at the uncomplaining patience of the Saviour. He did not doubt that the sight of this Man, in contrast with Barabbas, would move the Jews to sympathy. But he did not understand the fanatical hatred of the priests for Him, who, as the Light of the world, had made manifest their darkness and error. They had moved the mob to a mad fury, and again priests, rulers, and people raised that awful cry, "Crucify Him, crucify Him." At last, losing all patience with their unreasoning cruelty, Pilate cried out despairingly, "Take ye Him, and crucify Him: for I find no fault in Him."

The Roman governor, though familiar with cruel scenes, was moved with sympathy for the suffering prisoner, who, condemned and scourged, with bleeding brow and lacerated back, still had the bearing of a king upon his throne. But the priests declared, "We have a law, and by our law He ought to die, because He made Himself the Son of God."

Pilate was startled. He had no correct idea of Christ and His mission; but he had an indistinct faith in God and in beings superior to humanity. A thought that had once before passed through his mind now took more definite shape. He questioned whether it might not be a divine being that stood before him, clad in the purple robe of mockery, and crowned with thorns.

Again he went into the judgment hall, and said to Jesus, "Whence art Thou?" But Jesus gave him no answer. The Saviour had spoken freely to Pilate, explaining His own mission as a witness to the truth. Pilate had disregarded the light. He had abused the high office of judge by yielding his principles and authority to the demands of the mob. Jesus had no further light for him. Vexed at His silence, Pilate said haughtily:

"Speakest Thou not unto me? knowest Thou not that I have power to crucify Thee, and have power to release Thee?"

Jesus answered, "Thou couldest have no power at all against Me, except it were given thee from above: therefore he that delivered Me unto thee hath the greater sin."

Thus the pitying Saviour, in the midst of His intense suffering and grief, excused as far as possible the act of the Roman governor who gave Him up to be crucified. What a scene was this to hand down to the world for all time! What a light it sheds upon the character of Him who is the Judge of all the earth!

"He that delivered Me unto thee," said Jesus, "hath the greater sin." By this Christ meant Caiaphas, who, as high priest, represented the Jewish nation. They knew the principles that controlled the Roman authorities. They had had light in the prophecies that testified of Christ, and in His own teachings and miracles. The Jewish judges had received unmistakable evidence of the divinity of Him whom they condemned to death. And according to their light would they be judged.

The greatest guilt and heaviest responsibility belonged to those who stood in the highest places in the nation, the depositaries of sacred trusts that they were basely betraying. Pilate, Herod, and the Roman soldiers were comparatively ignorant of Jesus. They thought to please the priests and rulers by abusing Him. They had not the light which the Jewish nation had so abundantly received. Had the light been given to the soldiers, they would not have treated Christ as cruelly as they did.

Again Pilate proposed to release the Saviour. "But the Jews cried out, saying, If thou let this man go, thou art not Caesar's friend." Thus these hypocrites pretended to be jealous for the authority of Caesar. Of all the opponents of the Roman rule, the Jews were most bitter. When it was safe for them to do so, they were most tyrannical in enforcing their own national and religious requirements; but when they desired to bring about some purpose of cruelty, they exalted the power of Caesar. To accomplish the destruction of Christ, they would profess loyalty to the foreign rule which they hated.

"Whosoever maketh himself a king," they continued, "speaketh against Caesar." This was touching Pilate in a weak point. He was under suspicion by the Roman government, and he knew that such a report would be ruin to him. He knew that if the Jews were thwarted, their rage would be turned against him. They would leave nothing undone to accomplish their revenge. He had before him an example of the persistence with which they sought the life of One whom they hated without reason.

Pilate then took his place on the judgment seat, and again presented Jesus to the people, saying, "Behold your King!" Again the mad cry was heard, "Away with Him, crucify Him." In a voice that was heard far and near, Pilate asked, "Shall I crucify your King?" But from profane, blasphemous lips went forth the words, "We have no king but Caesar."

Thus by choosing a heathen ruler, the Jewish nation had withdrawn from the theocracy. They had rejected God as their king. Henceforth they had no deliverer. They had no king but Caesar. To this the priests and teachers had led the people. For this, with the fearful results that followed, they were responsible. A nation's sin and a nation's ruin were due to the religious leaders.

"When Pilate saw that he could prevail nothing, but that rather a tumult was made, he took water, and washed his hands before the multitude, saying, I am innocent of the blood of this just Person: see ye to it." In fear and self-condemnation Pilate looked upon the Saviour. In the vast sea of upturned faces, His alone was peaceful. About His head a soft light seemed to shine. Pilate said in his heart, He is a God. Turning to the multitude he declared, I am clear of His blood. Take ye Him, and crucify Him. But mark ye, priests and rulers, I pronounce Him a just man. May He whom He claims as His Father judge you and not me for this day's work. Then to Jesus he said, Forgive me for this act; I cannot save You. And when he had again scourged Jesus, he delivered Him to be crucified.

Pilate longed to deliver Jesus. But he saw that he could not do this, and yet retain his own position and honor. Rather than lose his worldly power, he chose to sacrifice an innocent life. How many, to escape loss or suffering, in like manner sacrifice principle. Conscience and duty point one way, and self-interest points another. The current sets strongly in the wrong direction, and he who compromises with evil is swept away into the thick darkness of guilt.

Pilate yielded to the demands of the mob. Rather than risk losing his position, he delivered Jesus up to be crucified. But in spite of his precautions, the very thing he dreaded afterward came upon him. His honors were stripped from him, he was cast down from his high office, and, stung by remorse and wounded pride, not long after the crucifixion he ended his own life. So all who compromise with sin will gain only sorrow and ruin. "There is a way which seemeth right unto a man, but the end thereof are the ways of death." Prov. 14:12.

When Pilate declared himself innocent of the blood of Christ, Caiaphas answered defiantly, "His blood be on us, and on our children." The awful words were taken up by the priests and rulers, and echoed by the crowd in an inhuman roar of voices. The whole multitude answered and said, "His blood be on us, and on our children."

The people of Israel had made their choice. Pointing to Jesus they had said, "Not this man, but Barabbas." Barabbas, the robber and murderer, was the representative of Satan. Christ was the representative of God. Christ had been rejected; Barabbas had been chosen. Barabbas they were to have. In making this choice they accepted him who from the beginning was a liar and a murderer. Satan was their leader. As a nation they would act out his dictation. His works they would do. His rule they must endure. That people who chose Barabbas in the place of Christ were to feel the cruelty of Barabbas as long as time should last.

Looking upon the smitten Lamb of God, the Jews had cried, "His blood be on us, and on our children." That awful cry ascended to the throne of God. That sentence, pronounced upon themselves, was written in heaven. That prayer was heard. The blood of the Son of God was upon their children and their children's children, a perpetual curse.

Terribly was it realized in the destruction of Jerusalem. Terribly has it been manifested in the condition of the Jewish nation for eighteen hundred years,—a branch severed from the vine, a dead, fruitless branch, to be gathered up and burned. From land to land throughout the world, from century to century, dead, dead in trespasses and sins!

Terribly will that prayer be fulfilled in the great judgment day. When Christ shall come to the earth again, not as a prisoner surrounded by a rabble will men see Him. They will see Him then as heaven's King. Christ will come in His own glory, in the glory of His Father, and the glory of the holy angels. Ten thousand times ten thousand, and thousands of thousands of angels, the beautiful and triumphant sons of God, possessing surpassing loveliness and glory, will escort Him on His way. Then shall He sit upon the throne of His glory, and before Him shall be gathered all nations. Then every eye shall see Him, and they also that pierced Him. In the place of a crown of thorns, He will wear a crown of glory,—a crown within a crown. In place of that old purple kingly robe, He will be clothed in raiment of whitest white, "so as no fuller on earth can white them." Mark 9:3. And on His vesture and on His thigh a name will be written, "King of kings, and Lord of lords." Rev. 19:16. Those who mocked and smote Him will be there. The priests and rulers will behold again the scene in the judgment hall. Every circumstance will appear before them, as if written in letters of fire. Then those who prayed, "His blood be on us, and on our children," will receive the answer to their prayer. Then the whole world will know and understand. They will realize who and what they, poor, feeble, finite beings, have been warring against. In awful agony and horror they will cry to the mountains and rocks, "Fall on us, and hide us from the face of Him that sitteth on the throne, and from the wrath of the Lamb: for the great day of His wrath is come; and who shall be able to stand?" Rev. 6:16, 17.

FIVE

CALVARY

And when they were come to the place, which is called Calvary, there they crucified Him."

"That He might sanctify the people with His own blood," Christ "suffered without the gate." Heb. 13:12. For transgression of the law of God, Adam and Eve were banished from Eden. Christ, our substitute, was to suffer without the boundaries of Jerusalem. He died outside the gate, where felons and murderers were executed. Full of significance are the words, "Christ hath redeemed us from the curse of the law, being made a curse for us." Gal. 3:13.

A vast multitude followed Jesus from the judgment hall to Calvary. The news of His condemnation had spread throughout Jerusalem, and people of all classes and all ranks flocked toward the place of crucifixion. The priests and rulers had been bound by a promise not to molest Christ's followers if He Himself were delivered to them, and the disciples and believers from the city and the surrounding region joined the throng that followed the Saviour.

As Jesus passed the gate of Pilate's court, the cross which had been prepared for Barabbas was laid upon His bruised and bleeding shoulders. Two companions of Barabbas were to suffer death at the same time with Jesus, and upon them also crosses were placed. The Saviour's burden was too heavy for Him in His weak and suffering condition. Since the Passover supper with His disciples, He had taken neither food nor drink. He had agonized in the garden of Gethsemane in conflict with satanic agencies. He had endured the anguish of the betrayal, and had seen His disciples forsake Him and flee. He had been taken to Annas, then to Caiaphas, and then to Pilate. From Pilate

He had been sent to Herod, then sent again to Pilate. From insult to renewed insult, from mockery to mockery, twice tortured by the scourge,—all that night there had been scene after scene of a character to try the soul of man to the uttermost. Christ had not failed. He had spoken no word but that tended to glorify God. All through the disgraceful farce of a trial He had borne Himself with firmness and dignity. But when after the second scourging the cross was laid upon Him, human nature could bear no more. He fell fainting beneath the burden.

The crowd that followed the Saviour saw His weak and staggering steps, but they manifested no compassion. They taunted and reviled Him because He could not carry the heavy cross. Again the burden was laid upon Him, and again He fell fainting to the ground. His persecutors saw that it was impossible for Him to carry His burden farther. They were puzzled to find anyone who would bear the humiliating load. The Jews themselves could not do this, because the defilement would prevent them from keeping the Passover. None even of the mob that followed Him would stoop to bear the cross.

At this time a stranger, Simon a Cyrenian, coming in from the country, meets the throng. He hears the taunts and ribaldry of the crowd; he hears the words contemptuously repeated, Make way for the King of the Jews! He stops in astonishment at the scene; and as he expresses his compassion, they seize him and place the cross upon his shoulders.

Simon had heard of Jesus. His sons were believers in the Saviour, but he himself was not a disciple. The bearing of the cross to Calvary was a blessing to Simon, and he was ever after grateful for this providence. It led him to take upon himself the cross of Christ from choice, and ever cheerfully stand beneath its burden.

Not a few women are in the crowd that follow the Uncondemned to His cruel death. Their attention is fixed upon Jesus. Some of them have seen Him before. Some have carried to Him their sick and suffering ones. Some have themselves been healed. The story of the scenes that have taken place is related. They wonder at the hatred of the crowd toward Him for whom their own hearts are melting and ready to break. And notwithstanding the action of the maddened throng, and the angry words of the priests and rulers, these women give expression to their sympathy. As Jesus falls fainting beneath the cross, they break forth into mournful wailing.

This was the only thing that attracted Christ's attention. Although full of suffering, while bearing the sins of the world, He was not indifferent to the expression of grief. He looked upon these women with tender compassion. They were not believers in Him; He knew that they were not lamenting Him as one sent from God, but were moved by feelings of human pity. He did not despise their sympathy, but it awakened in His heart a deeper sympathy for them. "Daughters of Jerusalem," He said, "weep not for Me, but weep for yourselves, and for your children." From the scene before Him, Christ looked forward to the time of Jerusalem's destruction. In that terrible scene, many of those who were now weeping for Him were to perish with their children.

From the fall of Jerusalem the thoughts of Jesus passed to a wider judgment. In the destruction of the impenitent city He saw a symbol of the final destruction to come upon the world. He said, "Then shall they begin to say to the mountains, Fall on us; and to the hills, Cover us. For if they do these things in a green tree, what shall be done in the dry?" By the green tree, Jesus represented Himself, the innocent Redeemer. God suffered His wrath against transgression to fall on His beloved Son. Jesus was to be crucified for the sins of men. What suffering, then, would the sinner bear who continued in sin? All the impenitent and unbelieving would know a sorrow and misery that language would fail to express

Of the multitude that followed the Saviour to Calvary, many had attended Him with joyful hosannas and the waving of palm branches as He rode triumphantly into Jerusalem. But not a few who had then shouted His praise, because it was popular to do so, now swelled the cry of "Crucify Him, crucify Him." When Christ rode into Jerusalem, the hopes of the disciples had been raised to the highest pitch. They had pressed close about their Master, feeling that it was a high honor to be connected with Him. Now in His humiliation they followed Him at a distance. They were filled with grief, and bowed down with disappointed hopes. How were the words of Jesus verified: "All ye shall be offended because of Me this night: for it is written, I will smite the shepherd, and the sheep of the flock shall be scattered abroad." Matt. 26:31.

Arriving at the place of execution, the prisoners were bound to the instruments of torture. The two thieves wrestled in the hands of those who placed them on the cross; but Jesus made no resistance. The mother of Jesus, supported by John the beloved disciple, had followed the steps of her Son to Calvary. She had seen Him fainting under the burden of the cross, and had longed to place a supporting hand beneath His wounded head, and to bathe that brow which had once been pillowed upon her bosom. But she was not permitted this mournful privilege. With the disciples she still cherished the hope that Jesus would manifest His power, and deliver Himself from His enemies. Again her heart would sink as she recalled the words in which He had foretold the very scenes that were then taking place. As the thieves were bound to the cross, she looked on with agonizing suspense. Would He who had given life to the dead suffer Himself to be crucified? Would the Son of God suffer Himself to be thus cruelly slain? Must she give up her faith that Jesus was the Messiah? Must she witness His shame and sorrow, without even the privilege of ministering to Him in His distress? She saw His hands stretched upon the cross; the hammer and the nails were brought, and as the spikes were driven through the tender flesh, the heart-stricken disciples bore away from the cruel scene the fainting form of the mother of Jesus.

The Saviour made no murmur of complaint. His face remained calm and serene, but great drops of sweat stood upon His brow. There was no pitying hand to wipe the death dew from His face, nor words of sympathy and unchanging fidelity to stay His human heart. While the soldiers were doing their fearful work, Jesus prayed for His enemies, "Father, forgive them; for they know not what they do." His mind passed from His own suffering to the sin of His persecutors, and the terrible retribution that would be theirs. No curses were called down upon the soldiers who were handling Him so roughly. No vengeance was invoked upon the priests and rulers, who were gloating over the accomplishment of their purpose. Christ pitied them in their ignorance and guilt. He breathed only a plea for their forgiveness,—"for they know not what they do."

Had they known that they were putting to torture One who had come to save the sinful race from eternal ruin, they would have been seized with remorse and horror. But their ignorance did not remove their guilt; for it was their privilege to know and accept Jesus as their Saviour. Some of them would yet see their sin, and repent, and be converted. Some by their impenitence would make it an impossibility for the prayer of Christ to be answered for them. Yet, just the same, God's purpose was reaching its fulfillment. Jesus was earning the right to become the advocate of men in the Father's presence.

That prayer of Christ for His enemies embraced the world. It took in every sinner that had lived or should live, from the beginning of the world to the end of time. Upon all rests the guilt of crucifying the Son of God. To all, forgiveness is freely offered. "Whosoever will" may have peace with God, and inherit eternal life.

As soon as Jesus was nailed to the cross, it was lifted by strong men, and with great violence thrust into the place prepared for it. This caused the most intense agony to the Son of God. Pilate then wrote an inscription in Hebrew, Greek, and Latin, and placed it upon the cross, above the head of Jesus. It read, "Jesus of Nazareth the King of the Jews." This inscription irritated the Jews. In Pilate's court they had cried, "Crucify Him." "We have no king but Caesar." John 19:15. They had declared that whoever should acknowledge any other king was a traitor. Pilate wrote out the sentiment they had expressed. No offense was mentioned, except that Jesus was the King of the Jews. The inscription was a virtual acknowledgment of the allegiance of the Jews to the Roman power. It declared that whoever might claim to be the King of Israel would be judged by them worthy of death. The priests had overreached themselves. When they were plotting the death of Christ, Caiaphas had declared it expedient that one man should die to save the nation. Now their hypocrisy was revealed. In order to destroy Christ, they had been ready to sacrifice even their national existence.

The priests saw what they had done, and asked Pilate to change the inscription. They said, "Write not, The King of the Jews; but that He said, I am King of the Jews." But Pilate was angry with himself because of his former weakness, and he thoroughly despised the jealous and artful priests and rulers. He replied coldly, "What I have written I have written."

A higher power than Pilate or the Jews had directed the placing of that inscription above the head of Jesus. In the providence of God it was to awaken thought, and investigation of the Scriptures. The place where Christ was crucified was near to the city. Thousands of people from all lands were then at Jerusalem, and the inscription declaring Jesus of Nazareth the Messiah would come to their notice. It was a living truth, transcribed by a hand that God had guided.

In the sufferings of Christ upon the cross prophecy was fulfilled. Centuries before the crucifixion, the Saviour had foretold the treatment He was to receive. He said, "Dogs have compassed Me: the assembly of the wicked have enclosed Me: they pierced My hands and My feet. I may tell all My bones: they look and stare upon Me. They part My garments among them, and cast lots upon My vesture." Ps. 22:16-18. The prophecy concerning His garments was carried out without counsel or interference from the friends or the enemies of the Crucified One. To the soldiers who had placed Him upon the cross, His clothing was given. Christ heard the men's contention as they parted the garments among them. His tunic was woven throughout without seam, and they said, "Let us not rend it, but cast lots for it, whose it shall be."

In another prophecy the Saviour declared, "Reproach hath broken My heart; and I am full of heaviness: and I looked for some to take pity, but there was none; and for comforters, but I found none. They gave Me also gall for My meat; and in My thirst they gave Me vinegar to drink." Ps. 69:20, 21. To those who suffered death by the cross, it was permitted to give a stupefying potion, to deaden the sense of pain. This was offered to Jesus; but when He had tasted it, He refused it. He would receive nothing that could becloud His mind. His faith must keep fast hold upon God. This was His only strength. To becloud His senses would give Satan an advantage.

The enemies of Jesus vented their rage upon Him as He hung upon the cross. Priests, rulers, and scribes joined with the mob in mocking the dying Saviour. At the baptism and at the transfiguration the voice of God had been heard proclaiming Christ as His Son. Again, just before Christ's betrayal, the Father had spoken, witnessing to His divinity. But now the voice from heaven was silent. No testimony in Christ's favor was heard. Alone He suffered abuse and mockery from wicked men.

"If Thou be the Son of God," they said, "come down from the cross." "Let Him save Himself, if He be Christ, the chosen of God." In the wilderness of temptation Satan had declared, "If Thou be the Son of God, command that these stones be made bread." "If Thou be the Son of God, cast Thyself down" from the pinnacle of the temple. Matt. 4:3, 6. And Satan with his angels, in human form, was present at the cross. The archfiend and his hosts were co-operating with the priests and rulers. The teachers of the people had stimulated the ignorant mob to pronounce judgment against One upon whom many of them had never looked, until urged to bear testimony against Him. Priests, rulers, Pharisees, and the hardened rabble were confederated together in a satanic frenzy. Religious rulers united with Satan and his angels. They were doing his bidding.

Jesus, suffering and dying, heard every word as the priests declared, "He saved others; Himself He cannot save. Let Christ the King of Israel descend now from the cross, that we may see and believe." Christ could have come down from the cross. But it is because He would not save Himself that the sinner has hope of pardon and favor with God.

In their mockery of the Saviour, the men who professed to be the expounders of prophecy were repeating the very words which Inspiration had foretold they would utter upon this occasion. Yet in their blindness they did not see that they were fulfilling the prophecy. Those who in derision uttered the words, "He trusted in God; let Him deliver Him now, if He will have Him: for He said, I am the Son of God," little thought that their testimony would sound down the ages. But although spoken in mockery, these words led men to search the Scriptures as they had never done before. Wise men heard, searched, pondered, and prayed. There were those who never rested until, by comparing scripture with scripture, they saw the meaning of Christ's mission. Never before was there such a general knowledge of Jesus as when He hung upon the cross. Into the hearts of many who beheld the crucifixion scene, and who heard Christ's words, the light of truth was shining.

To Jesus in His agony on the cross there came one gleam of comfort. It was the prayer of the penitent thief. Both the men who were crucified with Jesus had at first railed upon Him; and one under his suffering only became more desperate and defiant. But not so with his companion. This man was not a hardened criminal; he had been led astray by evil associations, but he was less guilty than many of those who stood beside the cross reviling the Saviour. He had seen and heard Jesus, and had been convicted by His teaching, but he had been turned away from Him by the priests and rulers. Seeking to stifle conviction, he had plunged deeper and deeper into sin, until he was arrested, tried as a criminal, and condemned to die on the cross. In the judgment hall and on the way to Calvary he had been in company with Jesus. He had heard Pilate declare, "I find no fault in Him." John 19:4. He had marked His godlike bearing, and His pitying forgiveness of His tormentors. On the cross he sees the many great religionists shoot out the tongue with scorn, and ridicule the Lord Jesus. He sees the wagging heads. He hears the upbraiding speeches taken up by his companion in guilt: "If Thou be Christ, save Thyself and us." Among the passers-by he hears many defending Jesus. He hears them repeat

His words, and tell of His works. The conviction comes back to him that this is the Christ. Turning to his fellow criminal he says, "Dost not thou fear God, seeing thou art in the same condemnation?" The dying thieves have no longer anything to fear from man. But upon one of them presses the conviction that there is a God to fear, a future to cause him to tremble. And now, all sin-polluted as it is, his life history is about to close. "And we indeed justly," he moans; "for we receive the due reward of our deeds: but this Man hath done nothing amiss."

There is no question now. There are no doubts, no reproaches. When condemned for his crime, the thief had become hopeless and despairing; but strange, tender thoughts now spring up. He calls to mind all he has heard of Jesus, how He has healed the sick and pardoned sin. He has heard the words of those who believed in Jesus and followed Him weeping. He has seen and read the title above the Saviour's head. He has heard the passers-by repeat it, some with grieved, quivering lips, others with jesting and mockery. The Holy Spirit illuminates his mind, and little by little the chain of evidence is joined together. In Jesus, bruised, mocked, and hanging upon the cross, he sees the Lamb of God, that taketh away the sin of the world. Hope is mingled with anguish in his voice as the helpless, dying soul casts himself upon a dying Saviour. "Lord, remember me," he cries, "when Thou comest into Thy kingdom."

Quickly the answer came. Soft and melodious the tone, full of love, compassion, and power the words: Verily I say unto thee today, Thou shalt be with Me in paradise.

For long hours of agony, reviling and mockery have fallen upon the ears of Jesus. As He hangs upon the cross, there floats up to Him still the sound of jeers and curses. With longing heart He has listened for some expression of faith from His disciples. He has heard only the mournful words, "We trusted that it had been He which should have redeemed Israel." How grateful then to the Saviour was the utterance of faith and love from the dying thief! While the leading Jews deny Him, and even the disciples doubt His divinity, the poor thief, upon the brink of eternity, calls Jesus Lord. Many were ready to call Him

Lord when He wrought miracles, and after He had risen from the grave; but none acknowledged Him as He hung dying upon the cross save the penitent thief who was saved at the eleventh hour.

The bystanders caught the words as the thief called Jesus Lord. The tone of the repentant man arrested their attention. Those who at the foot of the cross had been quarreling over Christ's garments, and casting lots upon His vesture, stopped to listen. Their angry tones were hushed. With bated breath they looked upon Christ, and waited for the response from those dying lips.

As He spoke the words of promise, the dark cloud that seemed to enshroud the cross was pierced by a bright and living light. To the penitent thief came the perfect peace of acceptance with God. Christ in His humiliation was glorified. He who in all other eyes appeared to be conquered was a Conqueror. He was acknowledged as the Sin Bearer. Men may exercise power over His human body. They may pierce the holy temples with the crown of thorns. They may strip from Him His raiment, and quarrel over its division. But they cannot rob Him of His power to forgive sins. In dying He bears testimony to His own divinity and to the glory of the Father. His ear is not heavy that it cannot hear, neither His arm shortened that it cannot save. It is His royal right to save unto the uttermost all who come unto God by Him.

I say unto thee today, Thou shalt be with Me in Paradise. Christ did not promise that the thief should be with Him in Paradise that day. He Himself did not go that day to Paradise. He slept in the tomb, and on the morning of the resurrection He said, "I am not yet ascended to My Father." John 20:17. But on the day of the crucifixion, the day of apparent defeat and darkness, the promise was given. "Today" while dying upon the cross as a malefactor, Christ assures the poor sinner, Thou shalt be with Me in Paradise.

The thieves crucified with Jesus were placed "on either side one, and Jesus in the midst." This was done by the direction of the priests and rulers. Christ's position between the thieves was to indicate that He was the greatest criminal of the three. Thus was fulfilled the scripture, "He was numbered with the transgressors." Isa. 53:12. But the full meaning of their act the priests did not see. As Jesus, crucified with the thieves, was placed "in the midst," so His cross was placed in the midst of a world lying in sin. And the words of pardon spoken to the penitent thief kindled a light that will shine to the earth's remotest bounds.

With amazement the angels beheld the infinite love of Jesus, who, suffering the most intense agony of mind and body, thought only of others, and encouraged the penitent soul to believe. In His humiliation He as a prophet had addressed the daughters of Jerusalem; as priest and advocate He had pleaded with the Father to forgive His murderers; as a loving Saviour He had forgiven the sins of the penitent thief.

As the eyes of Jesus wandered over the multitude about Him, one figure arrested His attention. At the foot of the cross stood His mother, supported by the disciple John. She could not endure to remain away from her Son; and John, knowing that the end was near, had brought her again to the cross. In His dying hour, Christ remembered His mother. Looking into her grief-stricken face and then upon John, He said to her, "Woman, behold thy son!" then to John, "Behold thy mother!" John understood Christ's words, and accepted the trust. He at once took Mary to his home, and from that hour cared for her tenderly. O pitiful, loving Saviour; amid all His physical pain and mental anguish, He had a thoughtful care for His mother! He had no money with which to provide for her comfort; but He was enshrined in the heart of John, and He gave His mother to him as a precious legacy. Thus He provided for her that which she most needed,—the tender sympathy of one who loved her because she loved Jesus. And in receiving her as a sacred trust, John was receiving a great blessing. She was a constant reminder of his beloved Master.

The perfect example of Christ's filial love shines forth with undimmed luster from the mist of ages. For nearly thirty years Jesus by His daily toil had helped bear the burdens of the home. And now, even in His last agony, He remembers to provide for His sorrowing, widowed mother. The same spirit will be seen in every disciple of our

Lord. Those who follow Christ will feel that it is a part of their religion to respect and provide for their parents. From the heart where His love is cherished, father and mother will never fail of receiving thoughtful care and tender sympathy.

And now the Lord of glory was dying, a ransom for the race. In yielding up His precious life, Christ was not upheld by triumphant joy. All was oppressive gloom. It was not the dread of death that weighed upon Him. It was not the pain and ignominy of the cross that caused His inexpressible agony. Christ was the prince of sufferers; but His suffering was from a sense of the malignity of sin, a knowledge that through familiarity with evil, man had become blinded to its enormity. Christ saw how deep is the hold of sin upon the human heart, how few would be willing to break from its power. He knew that without help from God, humanity must perish, and He saw multitudes perishing within reach of abundant help.

Upon Christ as our substitute and surety was laid the iniquity of us all. He was counted a transgressor, that He might redeem us from the condemnation of the law. The guilt of every descendant of Adam was pressing upon His heart. The wrath of God against sin, the terrible manifestation of His displeasure because of iniquity, filled the soul of His Son with consternation. All His life Christ had been publishing to a fallen world the good news of the Father's mercy and pardoning love. Salvation for the chief of sinners was His theme. But now with the terrible weight of guilt He bears, He cannot see the Father's reconciling face. The withdrawal of the divine countenance from the Saviour in this hour of supreme anguish pierced His heart with a sorrow that can never be fully understood by man. So great was this agony that His physical pain was hardly felt.

Satan with his fierce temptations wrung the heart of Jesus. The Saviour could not see through the portals of the tomb. Hope did not present to Him His coming forth from the grave a conqueror, or tell Him of the Father's acceptance of the sacrifice. He feared that sin was so offensive to God that Their separation was to be eternal. Christ felt the anguish which the sinner will feel when mercy shall no longer plead for the guilty race. It was the sense of sin, bringing the Father's wrath upon Him as man's substitute, that made the cup He drank so bitter, and broke the heart of the Son of God.

With amazement angels witnessed the Saviour's despairing agony. The hosts of heaven veiled their faces from the fearful sight. Inanimate nature expressed sympathy with its insulted and dying Author. The sun refused to look upon the awful scene. Its full, bright rays were illuminating the earth at midday, when suddenly it seemed to be blotted out. Complete darkness, like a funeral pall, enveloped the cross. "There was darkness over all the land unto the ninth hour." There was no eclipse or other natural cause for this darkness, which was as deep as midnight without moon or stars. It was a miraculous testimony given by God that the faith of after generations might be confirmed.

In that thick darkness God's presence was hidden. He makes darkness His pavilion, and conceals His glory from human eyes. God and His holy angels were beside the cross. The Father was with His Son. Yet His presence was not revealed. Had His glory flashed forth from the cloud, every human beholder would have been destroyed. And in that dreadful hour Christ was not to be comforted with the Father's presence. He trod the wine press alone, and of the people there was none with Him.

In the thick darkness, God veiled the last human agony of His Son. All who had seen Christ in His suffering had been convicted of His divinity. That face, once beheld by humanity, was never forgotten. As the face of Cain expressed his guilt as a murderer, so the face of Christ revealed innocence, serenity, benevolence,—the image of God. But His accusers would not give heed to the signet of heaven. Through long hours of agony Christ had been gazed upon by the jeering multitude. Now He was mercifully hidden by the mantle of God.

The silence of the grave seemed to have fallen upon Calvary. A nameless terror held the throng that was gathered about the cross. The cursing and reviling ceased in the midst of half-uttered sentences. Men, women, and children fell prostrate upon the earth. Vivid lightnings occasionally flashed forth from the cloud, and revealed the cross and the crucified Redeemer. Priests, rulers, scribes, executioners, and the mob, all thought that their time of retribution had come. After a while some whispered that Jesus would now come down from the cross. Some attempted to grope their way back to the city, beating their breasts and wailing in fear.

At the ninth hour the darkness lifted from the people, but still enveloped the Saviour. It was a symbol of the agony and horror that weighed upon His heart. No eye could pierce the gloom that surrounded the cross, and none could penetrate the deeper gloom that enshrouded the suffering soul of Christ. The angry lightnings seemed to be hurled at Him as He hung upon the cross. Then "Jesus cried with a loud voice, saying, Eloi, Eloi, lama sabachthani?" "My God, My God, why hast Thou forsaken Me?" As the outer gloom settled about the Saviour, many voices exclaimed: The vengeance of heaven is upon Him. The bolts of God's wrath are hurled at Him, because He claimed to be the Son of God. Many who believed on Him heard His despairing cry. Hope left them. If God had forsaken Jesus, in what could His followers trust?

When the darkness lifted from the oppressed spirit of Christ, He revived to a sense of physical suffering, and said, "I thirst." One of the Roman soldiers, touched with pity as he looked at the parched lips, took a sponge on a stalk of hyssop, and dipping it in a vessel of vinegar, offered it to Jesus. But the priests mocked at His agony. When darkness covered the earth, they had been filled with fear; as their terror abated, the dread returned that Jesus would yet escape them. His words, "Eloi, Eloi, lama sabachthani?" they had misinterpreted. With bitter contempt and scorn they said, "This man calleth for Elias." The last opportunity to relieve His sufferings they refused. "Let be," they said, "let us see whether Elias will come to save Him."

The spotless Son of God hung upon the cross, His flesh lacerated with stripes; those hands so often reached out in blessing, nailed to the wooden bars; those feet so tireless on ministries of love, spiked to the tree; that royal head pierced by the crown of thorns; those quivering lips shaped to the cry of woe. And all that He endured—the blood drops that flowed from His head, His hands, His feet, the agony that racked His frame, and the unutterable anguish that filled His soul at the hiding of His Father's face—speaks to each child of humanity, declaring, It is for thee that the Son of God consents to bear this burden of guilt; for thee He spoils the domain of death, and opens the gates of Paradise. He who stilled the angry waves and walked the foam-capped billows, who made devils tremble and disease flee, who opened blind eyes and called forth the dead to life,—offers Himself upon the cross as a sacrifice, and this from love to thee. He, the Sin Bearer, endures the wrath of divine justice, and for thy sake becomes sin itself.

In silence the beholders watched for the end of the fearful scene. The sun shone forth; but the cross was still enveloped in darkness. Priests and rulers looked toward Jerusalem; and lo, the dense cloud had settled over the city and the plains of Judea. The Sun of Righteousness, the Light of the world, was withdrawing His beams from the once favored city of Jerusalem. The fierce lightnings of God's wrath were directed against the fated city.

Suddenly the gloom lifted from the cross, and in clear, trumpetlike tones, that seemed to resound throughout creation, Jesus cried, "It is finished." "Father, into Thy hands I commend My spirit." A light encircled the cross, and the face of the Saviour shone with a glory like the sun. He then bowed His head upon His breast, and died.

Amid the awful darkness, apparently forsaken of God, Christ had drained the last dregs in the cup of human woe. In those dreadful hours He had relied upon the evidence of His Father's acceptance heretofore given Him. He was acquainted with the character of His Father; He understood His justice, His mercy, and His great love. By faith He rested in Him whom it had ever been His joy to obey. And as in submission He committed Himself to God, the sense of the loss of His Father's favor was withdrawn. By faith, Christ was victor.

Never before had the earth witnessed such a scene. The multitude stood paralyzed, and with bated breath gazed upon the Saviour. Again darkness settled upon the earth, and a hoarse rumbling, like heavy thunder, was heard. There was a violent earthquake. The people were shaken together in heaps. The wildest confusion and consternation ensued. In the surrounding mountains, rocks were rent asunder, and went crashing down into the plains. Sepulchers were broken open, and the dead were cast out of their tombs. Creation seemed to be shivering to atoms. Priests, rulers, soldiers, executioners, and people, mute with terror, lay prostrate upon the ground.

When the loud cry, "It is finished," came from the lips of Christ, the priests were officiating in the temple. It was the hour of the evening sacrifice. The lamb representing Christ had been brought to be slain. Clothed in his significant and beautiful dress, the priest stood with lifted knife, as did Abraham when he was about to slay his son. With intense interest the people were looking on. But the earth trembles and quakes; for the Lord Himself draws near. With a rending noise the inner veil of the temple is torn from top to bottom by an unseen hand, throwing open to the gaze of the multitude a place once filled with the presence of God. In this place the Shekinah had dwelt. Here God had manifested His glory above the mercy seat. No one but the high priest ever lifted the veil separating this apartment from the rest of the temple. He entered in once a year to make an atonement for the sins of the people. But lo, this veil is rent in twain. The most holy place of the earthly sanctuary is no longer sacred.

All is terror and confusion. The priest is about to slay the victim; but the knife drops from his nerveless hand, and the lamb escapes. Type has met antitype in the death of God's Son. The great sacrifice has been made. The way into the holiest is laid open. A new and living way is prepared for all. No longer need sinful, sorrowing humanity await the coming of the high priest. Henceforth the Saviour was to officiate as priest and advocate in the heaven of heavens. It was as if a living voice had spoken to the worshipers: There is now an end to all sacrifices and offerings for sin. The Son of God is come according to His word, "Lo, I come (in the volume of the Book it is written of Me,) to do Thy will, O God." "By His own blood" He entereth "in once into the holy place, having obtained eternal redemption for us." Heb. 10:7; 9:12.

SIX

"IT IS FINISHED"

Christ did not yield up His life till He had accomplished the work which He came to do, and with His parting breath He exclaimed, "It is finished." John 19:30. The battle had been won. His right hand and His holy arm had gotten Him the victory. As a Conqueror He planted His banner on the eternal heights. Was there not joy among the angels? All heaven triumphed in the Saviour's victory. Satan was defeated, and knew that his kingdom was lost.

To the angels and the unfallen worlds the cry, "It is finished," had a deep significance. It was for them as well as for us that the great work of redemption had been accomplished. They with us share the fruits of Christ's victory.

Not until the death of Christ was the character of Satan clearly revealed to the angels or to the unfallen worlds. The archapostate had so clothed himself with deception that even holy beings had not understood his principles. They had not clearly seen the nature of his rebellion.

It was a being of wonderful power and glory that had set himself against God. Of Lucifer the Lord says, "Thou sealest up the sum, full of wisdom, and perfect in beauty." Ezek. 28:12. Lucifer had been the covering cherub. He had stood in the light of God's presence. He had been the highest of all created beings, and had been foremost in revealing God's purposes to the universe. After he had sinned, his power to deceive was the more deceptive, and the unveiling of his character was the more difficult, because of the exalted position he had held with the Father.

God could have destroyed Satan and his sympathizers as easily as one can cast a pebble to the earth; but He did not do this. Rebellion was not to be overcome by force. Compelling power is found only under Satan's government. The Lord's principles are not of this order. His authority rests upon goodness, mercy, and love; and the presentation of these principles is the means to be used. God's government is moral, and truth and love are to be the prevailing power.

It was God's purpose to place things on an eternal basis of security, and in the councils of heaven it was decided that time must be given for Satan to develop the principles which were the foundation of his system of government. He had claimed that these were superior to God's principles. Time was given for the working of Satan's principles, that they might be seen by the heavenly universe.

Satan led men into sin, and the plan of redemption was put in operation. For four thousand years, Christ was working for man's uplifting, and Satan for his ruin and degradation. And the heavenly universe beheld it all.

When Jesus came into the world, Satan's power was turned against Him. From the time when He appeared as a babe in Bethlehem, the usurper worked to bring about His destruction. In every possible way he sought to prevent Jesus from developing a perfect childhood, a faultless manhood, a holy ministry, and an unblemished sacrifice. But he was defeated. He could not lead Jesus into sin. He could not discourage Him, or drive Him from a work He had come on earth to do. From the desert to Calvary, the storm of Satan's wrath beat upon Him, but the more mercilessly it fell, the more firmly did the Son of God cling to the hand of His Father, and press on in the bloodstained path. All the efforts of Satan to oppress and overcome Him only brought out in a purer light His spotless character.

All heaven and the unfallen worlds had been witnesses to the controversy. With what intense interest did they follow the closing scenes of the conflict. They beheld the Saviour enter the garden of Gethsemane, His soul bowed down with the horror of a great darkness. They heard His bitter cry, "Father, if it be possible, let this cup pass from Me." Matt. 26:39. As the Father's presence was withdrawn, they saw Him sorrowful with a bitterness of sorrow exceeding that of the last great struggle with death. The bloody sweat was forced from His pores, and fell in drops upon the ground. Thrice the prayer for deliverance was wrung from His lips. Heaven could no longer endure the sight, and a messenger of comfort was sent to the Son of God.

Heaven beheld the Victim betrayed into the hands of the murderous mob, and with mockery and violence hurried from one tribunal to another. It heard the sneers of His persecutors because of His lowly birth. It heard the denial with cursing and swearing by one of His best-loved disciples. It saw the frenzied work of Satan, and his power over the hearts of men. Oh, fearful scene! the Saviour seized at midnight in Gethsemane, dragged to and fro from palace to judgment hall, arraigned twice before the priests, twice before the Sanhedrin, twice before Pilate, and once before Herod, mocked, scourged, condemned, and led out to be crucified, bearing the heavy burden of the cross, amid the wailing of the daughters of Jerusalem and the jeering of the rabble.

Heaven viewed with grief and amazement Christ hanging upon the cross, blood flowing from His wounded temples, and sweat tinged with blood standing upon His brow. From His hands and feet the blood fell, drop by drop, upon the rock drilled for the foot of the cross. The wounds made by the nails gaped as the weight of His body dragged upon His hands. His labored breath grew quick and deep, as His soul panted under the burden of the sins of the world. All heaven was filled with wonder when the prayer of Christ was offered in the midst of His terrible suffering,—"Father, forgive them; for they know not what they do." Luke 23:34. Yet there stood men, formed in the image of God, joining to crush out the life of His only-begotten Son. What a sight for the heavenly universe!

The principalities and powers of darkness were assembled around the cross, casting the hellish shadow of unbelief into the hearts of men. When the Lord created these beings to stand before His throne, they were beautiful and glorious. Their loveliness and holiness were in accordance with their exalted station. They were enriched with the wisdom of God, and girded with the panoply of heaven. They were

Jehovah's ministers. But who could recognize in the fallen angels the glorious seraphim that once ministered in the heavenly courts?

Satanic agencies confederated with evil men in leading the people to believe Christ the chief of sinners, and to make Him the object of detestation. Those who mocked Christ as He hung upon the cross were imbued with the spirit of the first great rebel. He filled them with vile and loathsome speeches. He inspired their taunts. But by all this he gained nothing.

Could one sin have been found in Christ, had He in one particular yielded to Satan to escape the terrible torture, the enemy of God and man would have triumphed. Christ bowed His head and died, but He held fast His faith and His submission to God. "And I heard a loud voice saying in heaven, Now is come salvation, and strength, and the kingdom of our God, and the power of His Christ: for the accuser of our brethren is cast down, which accused them before our God day and night." Rev. 12:10.

Satan saw that his disguise was torn away. His administration was laid open before the unfallen angels and before the heavenly universe. He had revealed himself as a murderer. By shedding the blood of the Son of God, he had uprooted himself from the sympathies of the heavenly beings. Henceforth his work was restricted. Whatever attitude he might assume, he could no longer await the angels as they came from the heavenly courts, and before them accuse Christ's brethren of being clothed with the garments of blackness and the defilement of sin. The last link of sympathy between Satan and the heavenly world was broken.

Yet Satan was not then destroyed. The angels did not even then understand all that was involved in the great controversy. The principles at stake were to be more fully revealed. And for the sake of man, Satan's existence must be continued. Man as well as angels must see the contrast between the Prince of light and the prince of darkness. He must choose whom he will serve.

In the opening of the great controversy, Satan had declared that the law of God could not be obeyed, that justice was inconsistent with mercy, and that, should the law be broken, it would be impossible for the sinner to be pardoned. Every sin must meet its punishment, urged Satan; and if God should remit the punishment of sin, He would not be a God of truth and justice. When men broke the law of God, and defied His will, Satan exulted. It was proved, he declared, that the law could not be obeyed; man could not be forgiven. Because he, after his rebellion, had been banished from heaven, Satan claimed that the human race must be forever shut out from God's favor. God could not be just, he urged, and yet show mercy to the sinner.

But even as a sinner, man was in a different position from that of Satan. Lucifer in heaven had sinned in the light of God's glory. To him as to no other created being was given a revelation of God's love. Understanding the character of God, knowing His goodness, Satan chose to follow his own selfish, independent will. This choice was final. There was no more that God could do to save him. But man was deceived; his mind was darkened by Satan's sophistry. The height and depth of the love of God he did not know. For him there was hope in a knowledge of God's love. By beholding His character he might be drawn back to God.

Through Jesus, God's mercy was manifested to men; but mercy does not set aside justice. The law reveals the attributes of God's character, and not a jot or tittle of it could be changed to meet man in his fallen condition. God did not change His law, but He sacrificed Himself, in Christ, for man's redemption. "God was in Christ, reconciling the world unto Himself." 2 Cor. 5:19.

The law requires righteousness,—a righteous life, a perfect character; and this man has not to give. He cannot meet the claims of God's holy law. But Christ, coming to the earth as man, lived a holy life, and developed a perfect character. These He offers as a free gift to all who will receive them. His life stands for the life of men. Thus they have remission of sins that are past, through the forbearance of God. More than this, Christ imbues men with the attributes of God. He builds up the human character after the similitude of the divine character, a goodly fabric of spiritual strength and beauty. Thus the very righteousness of the law is fulfilled in the believer in Christ. God can "be just, and the justifier of him which believeth in Jesus." Rom. 3:26.

God's love has been expressed in His justice no less than in His mercy. Justice is the foundation of His throne, and the fruit of His love. It had been Satan's purpose to divorce mercy from truth and justice. He sought to prove that the righteousness of God's law is an enemy to peace. But Christ shows that in God's plan they are indissolubly joined together; the one cannot exist without the other. "Mercy and truth are met together; righteousness and peace have kissed each other." Ps. 85:10.

By His life and His death, Christ proved that God's justice did not destroy His mercy, but that sin could be forgiven, and that the law is righteous, and can be perfectly obeyed. Satan's charges were refuted. God had given man unmistakable evidence of His love.

Another deception was now to be brought forward. Satan declared that mercy destroyed justice, that the death of Christ abrogated the Father's law. Had it been possible for the law to be changed or abrogated, then Christ need not have died. But to abrogate the law would be to immortalize transgression, and place the world under Satan's control. It was because the law was changeless, because man could be saved only through obedience to its precepts, that Jesus was lifted up on the cross. Yet the very means by which Christ established the law Satan represented as destroying it. Here will come the last conflict of the great controversy between Christ and Satan.

That the law which was spoken by God's own voice is faulty, that some specification has been set aside, is the claim which Satan now puts forward. It is the last great deception that he will bring upon the world. He needs not to assail the whole law; if he can lead men to disregard one precept, his purpose is gained. For "whosoever shall keep the whole law, and yet offend in one point, he is guilty of all." James 2:10. By consenting to break one precept, men are brought under Satan's power. By substituting human law for God's law, Satan will seek to control the world. This work is foretold in prophecy. Of the great apostate power which is the representative of Satan, it is declared, "He shall speak great words against the Most High, and shall wear out the saints of the Most High, and think to change times and laws: and they shall be given into his hand." Dan. 7:25.

Men will surely set up their laws to counterwork the laws of God. They will seek to compel the consciences of others, and in their zeal to enforce these laws they will oppress their fellow men.

The warfare against God's law, which was begun in heaven, will be continued until the end of time. Every man will be tested. Obedience or disobedience is the question to be decided by the whole world. All will be called to choose between the law of God and the laws of men. Here the dividing line will be drawn. There will be but two classes. Every character will be fully developed; and all will show whether they have chosen the side of loyalty or that of rebellion.

Then the end will come. God will vindicate His law and deliver His people. Satan and all who have joined him in rebellion will be cut off. Sin and sinners will perish, root and branch, (Mal. 4:1),—Satan the root, and his followers the branches. The word will be fulfilled to the prince of evil, "Because thou hast set thine heart as the heart of God; . . . I will destroy thee, O covering cherub, from the midst of the stones of fire. . . . Thou shalt be a terror, and never shalt thou be any more." Then "the wicked shall not be: yea, thou shalt diligently consider his place, and it shall not be;" "they shall be as though they had not been." Ezek. 28:6-19; Ps. 37:10; Obadiah 16.

This is not an act of arbitrary power on the part of God. The rejecters of His mercy reap that which they have sown. God is the fountain of life; and when one chooses the service of sin, he separates from God, and thus cuts himself off from life. He is "alienated from the life of God." Christ says, "All they that hate Me love death." Eph. 4:18; Prov. 8:36. God gives them existence for a time that they may develop their character and reveal their principles. This accomplished, they receive the results of their own choice. By a life of rebellion, Satan and all who unite with him place themselves so out of harmony with God that His very presence is to them a consuming fire. The glory of Him who is love will destroy them.

At the beginning of the great controversy, the angels did not understand this. Had Satan and his host then been left to reap the full result of their sin, they would have perished; but it would not have been apparent to heavenly beings that this was the inevitable result of sin. A doubt of God's goodness would have remained in their minds as evil seed, to produce its deadly fruit of sin and woe.

But not so when the great controversy shall be ended. Then, the plan of redemption having been completed, the character of God is revealed to all created intelligences. The precepts of His law are seen to be perfect and immutable. Then sin has made manifest its nature, Satan his character. Then the extermination of sin will vindicate God's love and establish His honor before a universe of beings who delight to do His will, and in whose heart is His law.

Well, then, might the angels rejoice as they looked upon the Saviour's cross; for though they did not then understand all, they knew that the destruction of sin and Satan was forever made certain, that the redemption of man was assured, and that the universe was made eternally secure. Christ Himself fully comprehended the results of the sacrifice made upon Calvary. To all these He looked forward when upon the cross He cried out, "It is finished."

SEVEN

IN JOSEPH'S TOMB

A t last Jesus was at rest. The long day of shame and torture was ended. As the last rays of the setting sun ushered in the Sabbath, the Son of God lay in quietude in Joseph's tomb. His work completed, His hands folded in peace, He rested through the sacred hours of the Sabbath day.

In the beginning the Father and the Son had rested upon the Sabbath after Their work of creation. When "the heavens and the earth were finished, and all the host of them" (Gen. 2:1), the Creator and all heavenly beings rejoiced in contemplation of the glorious scene. "The morning stars sang together, and all the sons of God shouted for joy." Job 38:7. Now Jesus rested from the work of redemption; and though there was grief among those who loved Him on earth, yet there was joy in heaven. Glorious to the eyes of heavenly beings was the promise of the future. A restored creation, a redeemed race, that having conquered sin could never fall,—this, the result to flow from Christ's completed work, God and angels saw. With this scene the day upon which Jesus rested is forever linked. For "His work is perfect;" and "whatsoever God doeth, it shall be forever." Deut. 32:4; Eccl. 3:14. When there shall be a "restitution of all things, which God hath spoken by the mouth of all His holy prophets since the world began" (Acts 3:21), the creation Sabbath, the day on which Jesus lay at rest in Joseph's tomb, will still be a day of rest and rejoicing. Heaven and earth will unite in praise, as "from one Sabbath to another" (Isa. 66:23) the nations of the saved shall bow in joyful worship to God and the Lamb.

In the closing events of the crucifixion day, fresh evidence was given of the fulfillment of prophecy, and new witness borne to Christ's divinity. When the darkness had lifted from the cross, and the Saviour's dying cry had been uttered, immediately another voice was heard, saying, "Truly this was the Son of God." Matt. 27:54.

These words were said in no whispered tones. All eyes were turned to see whence they came. Who had spoken? It was the centurion, the Roman soldier. The divine patience of the Saviour, and His sudden death, with the cry of victory upon His lips, had impressed this heathen. In the bruised, broken body hanging upon the cross, the centurion recognized the form of the Son of God. He could not refrain from confessing his faith. Thus again evidence was given that our Redeemer was to see of the travail of His soul. Upon the very day of His death, three men, differing widely from one another, had declared their faith,—he who commanded the Roman guard, he who bore the cross of the Saviour, and he who died upon the cross at His side.

As evening drew on, an unearthly stillness hung over Calvary. The crowd dispersed, and many returned to Jerusalem greatly changed in spirit from what they had been in the morning. Many had flocked to the crucifixion from curiosity, and not from hatred toward Christ. Still they believed the accusations of the priests, and looked upon Christ as a malefactor. Under an unnatural excitement they had united with the mob in railing against Him. But when the earth was wrapped in blackness, and they stood accused by their own consciences, they felt guilty of a great wrong. No jest or mocking laughter was heard in the midst of that fearful gloom; and when it was lifted, they made their way to their homes in solemn silence. They were convinced that the charges of the priests were false, that Jesus was no pretender; and a few weeks later, when Peter preached upon the day of Pentecost, they were among the thousands who became converts to Christ.

But the Jewish leaders were unchanged by the events they had witnessed. Their hatred of Jesus had not abated. The darkness that had mantled the earth at the crucifixion was not more dense than that which still enveloped the minds of the priests and rulers. At His birth the star had known Christ, and had guided the wise men to the manger where He lay. The heavenly hosts had known Him, and had sung His praise over the plains of Bethlehem. The sea had known His voice, and had obeyed His command. Disease and death had recognized His authority, and had yielded to Him their prey. The sun had known Him, and at the sight of His dying anguish, had hidden its face of light. The rocks had known Him, and had shivered into fragments at His cry. Inanimate nature had known Christ, and had borne witness to His divinity. But the priests and rulers of Israel knew not the Son of God.

Yet the priests and rulers were not at rest. They had carried out their purpose in putting Christ to death; but they did not feel the sense of victory they had expected. Even in the hour of their apparent triumph, they were harassed with doubts as to what would next take place. They had heard the cry, "It is finished." "Father, into Thy hands I commend My spirit." John 19:30; Luke 23:46. They had seen the rocks rent, and had felt the mighty earthquake, and they were restless and uneasy.

They had been jealous of Christ's influence with the people when living; they were jealous of Him even in death. They dreaded the dead Christ more, far more, than they had ever feared the living Christ. They dreaded to have the attention of the people directed any further to the events attending His crucifixion. They feared the results of that day's work. Not on any account would they have had His body remain on the cross during the Sabbath. The Sabbath was now drawing on, and it would be a violation of its sanctity for the bodies to hang upon the cross. So, using this as a pretext, the leading Jews requested Pilate that the death of the victims might be hastened, and their bodies be removed before the setting of the sun.

Pilate was as unwilling as they for the body of Jesus to remain upon the cross. His consent having been obtained, the legs of the two thieves were broken to hasten their death; but Jesus was found to be already dead. The rude soldiers had been softened by what they had heard and seen of Christ, and they were restrained from breaking His limbs. Thus in the offering of the Lamb of God was fulfilled the law of the Passover, "They shall leave none of it unto the morning, nor break any bone of it: according to all the ordinances of the Passover they shall keep it." Num. 9:12

The priests and rulers were amazed to find that Christ was dead. Death by the cross was a lingering process; it was difficult to determine when life had ceased. It was an unheard-of thing for one to die within six hours of crucifixion. The priests wished to make sure of the death of Jesus, and at their suggestion a soldier thrust a spear into the Saviour's side. From the wound thus made, there flowed two copious and distinct streams, one of blood, the other of water. This was noted by all the beholders, and John states the occurrence very definitely. He says, "One of the soldiers with a spear pierced His side, and forthwith came there out blood and water. And he that saw it bare record, and his record is true: and he knoweth that he saith true, that ye might believe. For these things were done, that the scripture should be fulfilled, A bone of Him shall not be broken. And again another scripture saith, They shall look on Him whom they pierced." John 19:34-37.

After the resurrection the priests and rulers circulated the report that Christ did not die upon the cross, that He merely fainted, and was afterward revived. Another report affirmed that it was not a real body of flesh and bone, but the likeness of a body, that was laid in the tomb. The action of the Roman soldiers disproves these falsehoods. They broke not His legs, because He was already dead. To satisfy the priests, they pierced His side. Had not life been already extinct, this wound would have caused instant death.

But it was not the spear thrust, it was not the pain of the cross, that caused the death of Jesus. That cry, uttered "with a loud voice" (Matt. 27:50; Luke 23:46), at the moment of death, the stream of blood and water that flowed from His side, declared that He died of a broken heart. His heart was broken by mental anguish. He was slain by the sin of the world.

With the death of Christ the hopes of His disciples perished. They looked upon His closed eyelids and drooping head, His hair matted with blood, His pierced hands and feet, and their anguish was indescribable. Until the last they had not believed that He would die; they could hardly believe that He was really dead. Overwhelmed with sorrow, they did not recall His words foretelling this very scene. Nothing that He had said now gave them comfort. They saw only the cross and its bleeding Victim. The future seemed dark with despair. Their faith in Jesus had perished; but never had they loved their Lord as now. Never before had they so felt His worth, and their need of His presence.

Even in death, Christ's body was very precious to His disciples. They longed to give Him an honored burial, but knew not how to accomplish this. Treason against the Roman government was the crime for which Jesus was condemned, and persons put to death for this offense were consigned to a burial ground especially provided for such criminals. The disciple John with the women from Galilee had remained at the cross. They could not leave the body of their Lord to be handled by the unfeeling soldiers, and buried in a dishonored grave. Yet they could not prevent it. They could obtain no favors from the Jewish authorities, and they had no influence with Pilate.

In this emergency, Joseph of Arimathaea and Nicodemus came to the help of the disciples. Both these men were members of the Sanhedrin, and were acquainted with Pilate. Both were men of wealth and influence. They were determined that the body of Jesus should have an honorable burial.

Joseph went boldly to Pilate, and begged from him the body of Jesus. For the first time, Pilate learned that Jesus was really dead. Conflicting reports had reached him in regard to the events attending the crucifixion, but the knowledge of Christ's death had been purposely kept from him. Pilate had been warned by the priests and rulers against deception by Christ's disciples in regard to His body. Upon hearing Joseph's request, he therefore sent for the centurion who had charge at the cross, and learned for a certainty of the death of Jesus. He also drew from him an account of the scenes of Calvary, confirming the testimony of Joseph.

The request of Joseph was granted. While John was troubled about the burial of his Master, Joseph returned with Pilate's order for the body of Christ; and Nicodemus came bringing a costly mixture of myrrh and aloes, of about a hundred pounds' weight, for His embalming. The most honored in all Jerusalem could not have been shown more respect in death. The disciples were astonished to see these wealthy rulers as much interested as they themselves in the burial of their Lord.

Neither Joseph nor Nicodemus had openly accepted the Saviour while He was living. They knew that such a step would exclude them from the Sanhedrin, and they hoped to protect Him by their influence in its councils. For a time they had seemed to succeed; but the wily priests, seeing their favor to Christ, had thwarted their plans. In their absence Jesus had been condemned and delivered to be crucified. Now that He was dead, they no longer concealed their attachment to Him. While the disciples feared to show themselves openly as His followers, Joseph and Nicodemus came boldly to their aid. The help of these rich and honored men was greatly needed at this time. They could do for their dead Master what it was impossible for the poor disciples to do; and their wealth and influence protected them, in a great measure, from the malice of the priests and rulers.

Gently and reverently they removed with their own hands the body of Jesus from the cross. Their tears of sympathy fell fast as they looked upon His bruised and lacerated form. Joseph owned a new tomb, hewn in a rock. This he was reserving for himself; but it was near Calvary, and he now prepared it for Jesus. The body, together with the spices brought by Nicodemus, was carefully wrapped in a linen sheet, and the Redeemer was borne to the tomb. There the three disciples straightened the mangled limbs, and folded the bruised hands upon the pulseless breast. The Galilean women came to see that all had been done that could be done for the lifeless form of their beloved Teacher. Then they saw the heavy stone rolled against the entrance of the tomb, and the Saviour was left at rest. The women were last at the cross, and last at the tomb of Christ. While the evening shades were gathering, Mary Magdalene and the other Marys lingered about the resting place of their Lord, shedding tears of sorrow over the fate of Him whom they loved. "And they returned, . . . and rested the Sabbath day according to the commandment." Luke 23:56.

That was a never-to-be-forgotten Sabbath to the sorrowing disciples, and also to the priests, rulers, scribes, and people. At the setting of the sun on the evening of the preparation day the trumpets sounded, signifying that the Sabbath had begun. The Passover was observed as it had been for centuries, while He to whom it pointed had been slain by wicked hands, and lay in Joseph's tomb. On the Sabbath the courts of the temple were filled with worshipers. The high priest from Golgotha was there, splendidly robed in his sacerdotal garments. White-turbaned priests, full of activity, performed their duties. But some present were not at rest as the blood of bulls and goats was offered for sin. They were not conscious that type had met antitype, that an infinite sacrifice had been made for the sins of the world. They knew not that there was no further value in the performance of the ritual service. But never before had that service been witnessed with such conflicting feelings. The trumpets and musical instruments and the voices of the singers were as loud and clear as usual. But a sense of strangeness pervaded everything. One after another inquired about a strange event that had taken place. Hitherto the most holy place had been sacredly guarded from intrusion. But now it was open to all eyes. The heavy veil of tapestry, made of pure linen, and beautifully wrought with gold, scarlet, and purple, was rent from top to bottom. The place where Jehovah had met with the high priest, to communicate His glory, the place that had been God's sacred audience chamber, lay open to every eye,—a place no longer recognized by the Lord. With gloomy presentiments the priests ministered before the altar. The uncovering of the sacred mystery of the most holy place filled them with dread of coming calamity.

Many minds were busy with thoughts started by the scenes of Calvary. From the crucifixion to the resurrection many sleepless eyes were constantly searching the prophecies, some to learn the full meaning of the feast they were then celebrating, some to find evidence that Jesus was not what He claimed to be; and others with sorrowful hearts were searching for proofs that He was the true Messiah. Though searching with different objects in view, all were convicted of the same truth,—that prophecy had been fulfilled in the events of the past few days, and that the Crucified One was the world's Redeemer. Many who at that time united in the service never again took part in the paschal rites. Many even of the priests were convicted of the true character of Jesus. Their searching of the prophecies had not been in vain, and after His resurrection they acknowledged Him as the Son of God.

Nicodemus, when he saw Jesus lifted up on the cross, remembered His words spoken by night in the Mount of Olives: "As Moses lifted up the serpent in the wilderness, even so must the Son of man be lifted up: that whosoever believeth in Him should not perish, but have eternal life." John 3:14, 15. On that Sabbath, when Christ lay in the grave, Nicodemus had opportunity for reflection. A clearer light now illuminated his mind, and the words which Jesus had spoken to him were no longer mysterious. He felt that he had lost much by not connecting himself with the Saviour during His life. Now he recalled the events of Calvary. The prayer of Christ for His murderers and His answer to the petition of the dying thief spoke to the heart of the learned councilor. Again he looked upon the Saviour in His agony; again he heard that last cry, "It is finished," spoken like the words of a conqueror. Again he beheld the reeling earth, the darkened heavens, the rent veil, the shivered rocks, and his faith was forever established. The very event that destroyed the hopes of the disciples convinced Joseph and Nicodemus of the divinity of Jesus. Their fears were overcome by the courage of a firm and unwavering faith.

Never had Christ attracted the attention of the multitude as now that He was laid in the tomb. According to their practice, the people brought their sick and suffering ones to the temple courts, inquiring, Who can tell us of Jesus of Nazareth? Many had come from far to find Him who had healed the sick and raised the dead. On every side was heard the cry, We want Christ the Healer! Upon this occasion those who were thought to show indications of the leprosy were examined by the priests. Many were forced to hear their husbands, wives, or children pronounced leprous, and doomed to go forth from the shelter of their homes and the care of their friends, to warn off the stranger with the mournful cry, "Unclean, unclean!" The friendly hands of Jesus of Nazareth, that never refused to touch with healing the loathsome leper, were folded on His breast. The lips that had answered his petition with the comforting words, "I will; be thou clean" (Matt. 8:3), were now silent. Many appealed to the chief priests and rulers for sympathy and relief, but in vain. Apparently they were determined to have the living Christ among them again. With persistent earnestness they asked for Him. They would not be turned away. But they were driven from the temple courts, and soldiers were stationed at the gates to keep back the multitude that came with their sick and dying, demanding entrance.

The sufferers who had come to be healed by the Saviour sank under their disappointment. The streets were filled with mourning. The sick were dying for want of the healing touch of Jesus. Physicians were consulted in vain; there was no skill like that of Him who lay in Joseph's tomb.

The mourning cries of the suffering ones brought home to thousands of minds the conviction that a great light had gone out of the world. Without Christ, the earth was blackness and darkness. Many whose voices had swelled the cry of "Crucify Him, crucify Him," now realized the calamity that had fallen upon them, and would as eagerly have cried, Give us Jesus! had He still been alive.

When the people learned that Jesus had been put to death by the priests, inquiries were made regarding His death. The particulars of His trial were kept as private as possible; but during the time when He was in the grave, His name was on thousands of lips, and reports of His mock trial, and of the inhumanity of the priests and rulers, were circulated everywhere. By men of intellect these priests and rulers were called upon to explain the prophecies of the Old Testament concerning the Messiah, and while trying to frame some falsehood in reply, they became like men insane. The prophecies that pointed to

Christ's sufferings and death they could not explain, and many inquirers were convinced that the Scriptures had been fulfilled.

The revenge which the priests had thought would be so sweet was already bitterness to them. They knew that they were meeting the severe censure of the people; they knew that the very ones whom they had influenced against Jesus were now horrified by their own shameful work. These priests had tried to believe Jesus a deceiver; but it was in vain. Some of them had stood by the grave of Lazarus, and had seen the dead brought back to life. They trembled for fear that Christ would Himself rise from the dead, and again appear before them. They had heard Him declare that He had power to lay down His life and to take it again. They remembered that He had said, "Destroy this temple, and in three days I will raise it up." John 2:19. Judas had told them the words spoken by Jesus to the disciples while on the last journey to Jerusalem: "Behold, we go up to Jerusalem; and the Son of man shall be betrayed unto the chief priests and unto the scribes, and they shall condemn Him to death, and shall deliver Him to the Gentiles to mock, and to scourge, and to crucify Him: and the third day He shall rise again." Matt. 20:18, 19. When they heard these words, they had mocked and ridiculed. But now they remembered that Christ's predictions had so far been fulfilled. He had said that He would rise again the third day, and who could say that this also would not come to pass? They longed to shut out these thoughts, but they could not. Like their father, the devil, they believed and trembled.

Now that the frenzy of excitement was past, the image of Christ would intrude upon their minds. They beheld Him as He stood serene and uncomplaining before His enemies, suffering without a murmur their taunts and abuse. All the events of His trial and crucifixion came back to them with an overpowering conviction that He was the Son of God. They felt that He might at any time stand before them, the accused to become the accuser, the condemned to condemn, the slain to demand justice in the death of His murderers.

They could rest little upon the Sabbath. Though they would not step over a Gentile's threshold for fear of defilement, yet they held a council concerning the body of Christ. Death and the grave must hold Him whom they had crucified. "The chief priests and Pharisees came together unto Pilate, saying, Sir, we remember that that deceiver said, while He was yet alive, After three days I will rise again. Command therefore that the sepulcher be made sure until the third day, lest His disciples come by night, and steal Him away, and say unto the people, He is risen from the dead: so the last error shall be worse than the first. Pilate said unto them, Ye have a watch: go your way, make it as sure as ye can." Matt. 27:62-65.

The priests gave directions for securing the sepulcher. A great stone had been placed before the opening. Across this stone they placed cords, securing the ends to the solid rock, and sealing them with the Roman seal. The stone could not be moved without breaking the seal. A guard of one hundred soldiers was then stationed around the sepulcher to prevent it from being tampered with. The priests did all they could to keep Christ's body where it had been laid. He was sealed as securely in His tomb as if He were to remain there through all time.

So weak men counseled and planned. Little did these murderers realize the uselessness of their efforts. But by their action God was glorified. The very efforts made to prevent Christ's resurrection are the most convincing arguments in its proof. The greater the number of soldiers placed around the tomb, the stronger would be the testimony that He had risen. Hundreds of years before the death of Christ, the Holy Spirit had declared through the psalmist, "Why do the heathen rage, and the people imagine a vain thing? The kings of the earth set themselves, and the rulers take counsel together, against the Lord, and against His anointed. . . . He that sitteth in the heavens shall laugh: the Lord shall have them in derision." Ps. 2:1-4. Roman guards and Roman arms were powerless to confine the Lord of life within the tomb. The hour of His release was near.

EIGHT

"THE LORD IS RISEN"

The night of the first day of the week had worn slowly away. The darkest hour, just before daybreak, had come. Christ was still a prisoner in His narrow tomb. The great stone was in its place; the Roman seal was unbroken; the Roman guards were keeping their watch. And there were unseen watchers. Hosts of evil angels were gathered about the place. Had it been possible, the prince of darkness with his apostate army would have kept forever sealed the tomb that held the Son of God. But a heavenly host surrounded the sepulcher. Angels that excel in strength were guarding the tomb, and waiting to welcome the Prince of life.

"And, behold, there was a great earthquake: for the angel of the Lord descended from heaven." Clothed with the panoply of God, this angel left the heavenly courts. The bright beams of God's glory went before him, and illuminated his pathway. "His countenance was like lightning, and his raiment white as snow: and for fear of him the keepers did shake, and became as dead men."

Now, priests and rulers, where is the power of your guard? Brave soldiers that have never been afraid of human power are now as captives taken without sword or spear. The face they look upon is not the face of mortal warrior; it is the face of the mightiest of the Lord's host. This messenger is he who fills the position from which Satan fell. It is he who on the hills of Bethlehem proclaimed Christ's birth. The earth trembles at his approach, the hosts of darkness flee, and as he rolls away the stone, heaven seems to come down to the earth. The soldiers see him removing the stone as he would a pebble, and hear him cry, Son of God, come forth; Thy Father calls Thee. They see Jesus come forth from the grave, and hear Him proclaim over the rent sepulcher,

"I am the resurrection, and the life." As He comes forth in majesty and glory, the angel host bow low in adoration before the Redeemer, and welcome Him with songs of praise.

An earthquake marked the hour when Christ laid down His life, and another earthquake witnessed the moment when He took it up in triumph. He who had vanquished death and the grave came forth from the tomb with the tread of a conqueror, amid the reeling of the earth, the flashing of lightning, and the roaring of thunder. When He shall come to the earth again, He will shake "not the earth only, but also heaven." "The earth shall reel to and fro like a drunkard, and shall be removed like a cottage." "The heavens shall be rolled together as a scroll;" "the elements shall melt with fervent heat, the earth also and the works that are therein shall be burned up." But "the Lord will be the hope of His people, and the strength of the children of Israel." Heb. 12:26; Isa. 24:20; 34:4; 2 Peter 3:10; Joel 3:16.

At the death of Jesus the soldiers had beheld the earth wrapped in darkness at midday; but at the resurrection they saw the brightness of the angels illuminate the night, and heard the inhabitants of heaven singing with great joy and triumph: Thou hast vanquished Satan and the powers of darkness; Thou hast swallowed up death in victory!

Christ came forth from the tomb glorified, and the Roman guard beheld Him. Their eyes were riveted upon the face of Him whom they had so recently mocked and derided. In this glorified Being they beheld the prisoner whom they had seen in the judgment hall, the one for whom they had plaited a crown of thorns. This was the One who had stood unresisting before Pilate and Herod, His form lacerated by the cruel scourge. This was He who had been nailed to the cross, at whom the priests and rulers, full of self-satisfaction, had wagged their heads, saying, "He saved others; Himself He cannot save." Matt. 27:42. This was He who had been laid in Joseph's new tomb. The decree of heaven had loosed the captive. Mountains piled upon mountains over His sepulcher could not have prevented Him from coming forth.

At sight of the angels and the glorified Saviour the Roman guard had fainted and become as dead men. When the heavenly train was hidden from their view, they arose to their feet, and as quickly as their trembling limbs could carry them, made their way to the gate of the garden. Staggering like drunken men, they hurried on to the city, telling those whom they met the wonderful news. They were making their way to Pilate, but their report had been carried to the Jewish authorities, and the chief priests and rulers sent for them to be brought first into their presence. A strange appearance those soldiers presented. Trembling with fear, their faces colorless, they bore testimony to the resurrection of Christ. The soldiers told all, just as they had seen it; they had not had time to think or speak anything but the truth. With painful utterance they said, It was the Son of God who was crucified; we have heard an angel proclaiming Him as the Majesty of heaven, the King of glory.

The faces of the priests were as those of the dead. Caiaphas tried to speak. His lips moved, but they uttered no sound. The soldiers were about to leave the council room, when a voice stayed them. Caiaphas had at last found speech. Wait, wait, he said. Tell no one the things you have seen.

A lying report was then given to the soldiers. "Say ye," said the priests, "His disciples came by night, and stole Him away while we slept." Here the priests overreached themselves. How could the soldiers say that the disciples had stolen the body while they slept? If they were asleep, how could they know? And if the disciples had been proved guilty of stealing Christ's body, would not the priests have been first to condemn them? Or if the sentinels had slept at the tomb, would not the priests have been foremost in accusing them to Pilate?

The soldiers were horrified at the thought of bringing upon themselves the charge of sleeping at their post. This was an offense punishable with death. Should they bear false witness, deceiving the people, and placing their own lives in peril? Had they not kept their weary watch with sleepless vigilance? How could they stand the trial, even for the sake of money, if they perjured themselves?

In order to silence the testimony they feared, the priests promised to secure the safety of the guard, saying that Pilate would not desire to have such a report circulated any more than they did. The Roman soldiers sold their integrity to the Jews for money. They came in before the priests burdened with a most startling message of truth; they went out with a burden of money, and on their tongues a lying report which had been framed for them by the priests.

Meanwhile the report of Christ's resurrection had been carried to Pilate. Though Pilate was responsible for having given Christ up to die, he had been comparatively unconcerned. While he had condemned the Saviour unwillingly, and with a feeling of pity, he had felt no real compunction until now. In terror he now shut himself within his house, determined to see no one. But the priests made their way into his presence, told the story which they had invented, and urged him to overlook the sentinels' neglect of duty. Before consenting to this, he himself privately questioned the guard. They, fearing for their own safety, dared not conceal anything, and Pilate drew from them an account of all that had taken place. He did not prosecute the matter further, but from that time there was no peace for him.

When Jesus was laid in the grave, Satan triumphed. He dared to hope that the Saviour would not take up His life again. He claimed the Lord's body, and set his guard about the tomb, seeking to hold Christ a prisoner. He was bitterly angry when his angels fled at the approach of the heavenly messenger. When he saw Christ come forth in triumph, he knew that his kingdom would have an end, and that he must finally die.

The priests, in putting Christ to death, had made themselves the tools of Satan. Now they were entirely in his power. They were entangled in a snare from which they saw no escape but in continuing their warfare against Christ. When they heard the report of His resurrection, they feared the wrath of the people. They felt that their own lives were in danger. The only hope for them was to prove Christ an impostor by denying that He had risen. They bribed the soldiers, and secured Pilate's silence. They spread their lying reports far and near. But there were witnesses whom they could not silence. Many had heard of the soldiers' testimony to Christ's resurrection. And certain of the dead who came forth with Christ appeared to many, and declared that He had risen. Reports were brought to the priests of persons who had seen these risen ones, and heard their testimony. The priests and rulers were in continual dread, lest in walking the streets, or within the privacy of their own homes, they should come face to face with Christ. They felt that there was no safety for them. Bolts and bars were but poor protection against the Son of God. By day and by night that awful scene in the judgment hall, when they had cried, "His blood be on us, and on our children," was before them. Matt. 27:25. Nevermore would the memory of that scene fade from their minds. Nevermore would peaceful sleep come to their pillows.

When the voice of the mighty angel was heard at Christ's tomb, saying, Thy Father calls Thee, the Saviour came forth from the grave by the life that was in Himself. Now was proved the truth of His words, "I lay down My life, that I might take it again. . . . I have power to lay it down, and I have power to take it again." Now was fulfilled the prophecy He had spoken to the priests and rulers, "Destroy this temple, and in three days I will raise it up." John 10:17, 18; 2:19.

Over the rent sepulcher of Joseph, Christ had proclaimed in triumph, "I am the resurrection, and the life." These words could be spoken only by the Deity. All created beings live by the will and power of God. They are dependent recipients of the life of God. From the highest seraph to the humblest animate being, all are replenished from the Source of life. Only He who is one with God could say, I have power to lay down My life, and I have power to take it again. In His divinity, Christ possessed the power to break the bonds of death.

Christ arose from the dead as the first fruits of those that slept. He was the antitype of the wave sheaf, and His resurrection took place on the very day when the wave sheaf was to be presented before the Lord. For more than a thousand years this symbolic ceremony had been performed. From the harvest fields the first heads of ripened grain were gathered, and when the people went up to Jerusalem to the Passover, the sheaf of first fruits was waved as a thank offering before the Lord. Not until this was presented could the sickle be put to the grain, and it be gathered into sheaves. The sheaf dedicated to God represented the harvest. So Christ the first fruits represented the great spiritual harvest to be gathered for the kingdom of God. His resurrection is the type and pledge of the resurrection of all the righteous dead. "For if we believe that Jesus died and rose again, even so them also which sleep in Jesus will God bring with Him." 1 Thess. 4:14.

As Christ arose, He brought from the grave a multitude of captives. The earthquake at His death had rent open their graves, and when He arose, they came forth with Him. They were those who had been co-laborers with God, and who at the cost of their lives had borne testimony to the truth. Now they were to be witnesses for Him who had raised them from the dead.

During His ministry, Jesus had raised the dead to life. He had raised the son of the widow of Nain, and the ruler's daughter and Lazarus. But these were not clothed with immortality. After they were raised, they were still subject to death. But those who came forth from the grave at Christ's resurrection were raised to everlasting life. They ascended with Him as trophies of His victory over death and the grave. These, said Christ, are no longer the captives of Satan; I have redeemed them. I have brought them from the grave as the first fruits of My power, to be with Me where I am, nevermore to see death or experience sorrow.

These went into the city, and appeared unto many, declaring, Christ has risen from the dead, and we be risen with Him. Thus was immortalized the sacred truth of the resurrection. The risen saints bore witness to the truth of the words, "Thy dead men shall live, together with My dead body shall they arise." Their resurrection was an illustration of the fulfillment of the prophecy, "Awake and sing, ye that dwell in dust: for thy dew is as the dew of herbs, and the earth shall cast out the dead." Isa. 26:19. {DA 786.3}

To the believer, Christ is the resurrection and the life. In our Saviour the life that was lost through sin is restored; for He has life in Himself to quicken whom He will. He is invested with the right to give immortality. The life that He laid down in humanity, He takes up again, and gives to humanity. "I am come," He said, "that they might have life, and that they might have it more abundantly." "Whosoever drinketh of the water that I shall give him shall never thirst; but the water that I shall give him shall be in him a well of water springing up into everlasting life." "Whoso eateth My flesh, and drinketh My blood, hath eternal life; and I will raise him up at the last day." John 10:10; 4:14; 6:54.

To the believer, death is but a small matter. Christ speaks of it as if it were of little moment. "If a man keep My saying, he shall never see death," "he shall never taste of death." To the Christian, death is but a sleep, a moment of silence and darkness. The life is hid with Christ in God, and "when Christ, who is our life, shall appear, then shall ye also appear with Him in glory." John 8:51, 52; Col. 3:4.

The voice that cried from the cross, "It is finished," was heard among the dead. It pierced the walls of sepulchers, and summoned the sleepers to arise. Thus will it be when the voice of Christ shall be heard from heaven. That voice will penetrate the graves and unbar the tombs, and the dead in Christ shall arise. At the Saviour's resurrection a few graves were opened, but at His second coming all the precious dead shall hear His voice, and shall come forth to glorious, immortal life. The same power that raised Christ from the dead will raise His church, and glorify it with Him, above all principalities, above all powers, above every name that is named, not only in this world, but also in the world to come.

NINE

"WHY WEEPEST THOU?"

The women who had stood by the cross of Christ waited and watched for the hours of the Sabbath to pass. On the first day of the week, very early, they made their way to the tomb, taking with them precious spices to anoint the Saviour's body. They did not think about His rising from the dead. The sun of their hope had set, and night had settled down on their hearts. As they walked, they recounted Christ's works of mercy and His words of comfort. But they remembered not His words, "I will see you again." John 16:22.

Ignorant of what was even then taking place, they drew near the garden, saying as they went, "Who shall roll us away the stone from the door of the sepulcher?" They knew that they could not remove the stone, yet they kept on their way. And lo, the heavens were suddenly alight with glory that came not from the rising sun. The earth trembled. They saw that the great stone was rolled away. The grave was empty.

The women had not all come to the tomb from the same direction. Mary Magdalene was the first to reach the place; and upon seeing that the stone was removed, she hurried away to tell the disciples. Meanwhile the other women came up. A light was shining about the tomb, but the body of Jesus was not there. As they lingered about the place, suddenly they saw that they were not alone. A young man clothed in shining garments was sitting by the tomb. It was the angel who had rolled away the stone. He had taken the guise of humanity that he might not alarm these friends of Jesus. Yet about him the light of the heavenly glory was still shining, and the women were afraid. They turned to flee, but the angel's words stayed their steps. "Fear not ye," he said; "for I know that ye seek Jesus, which was crucified. He is not here: for He is risen, as He said. Come, see the place where the Lord lay. And go quickly, and tell His disciples that He is risen from the dead." Again they look into the tomb, and again they hear the wonderful news. Another angel in human form is there, and he says, "Why seek ye the living among the dead? He is not here, but is risen: remember how He spake unto you when He was yet in Galilee, saying, The Son of man must be delivered into the hands of sinful men, and be crucified, and the third day rise again."

He is risen, He is risen! The women repeat the words again and again. No need now for the anointing spices. The Saviour is living, and not dead. They remember now that when speaking of His death He said that He would rise again. What a day is this to the world! Quickly the women departed from the sepulcher "with fear and great joy; and did run to bring His disciples word."

Mary had not heard the good news. She went to Peter and John with the sorrowful message, "They have taken away the Lord out of the sepulcher, and we know not where they have laid Him." The disciples hurried to the tomb, and found it as Mary had said. They saw the shroud and the napkin, but they did not find their Lord. Yet even here was testimony that He had risen. The graveclothes were not thrown heedlessly aside, but carefully folded, each in a place by itself. John "saw, and believed." He did not yet understand the scripture that Christ must rise from the dead; but he now remembered the Saviour's words foretelling His resurrection.

It was Christ Himself who had placed those graveclothes with such care. When the mighty angel came down to the tomb, he was joined by another, who with his company had been keeping guard over the Lord's body. As the angel from heaven rolled away the stone, the other entered the tomb, and unbound the wrappings from the body of Jesus. But it was the Saviour's hand that folded each, and laid it in its place. In His sight who guides alike the star and the atom, there is nothing unimportant. Order and perfection are seen in all His work.

Mary had followed John and Peter to the tomb; when they returned to Jerusalem, she remained. As she looked into the empty tomb, grief filled her heart. Looking in, she saw the two angels, one at the head and the other at the foot where Jesus had lain. "Woman, why weepest thou?" they asked her. "Because they have taken away my Lord," she answered, "and I know not where they have laid Him."

Then she turned away, even from the angels, thinking that she must find someone who could tell her what had been done with the body of Jesus. Another voice addressed her, "Woman, why weepest thou? whom seekest thou?" Through her tear-dimmed eyes, Mary saw the form of a man, and thinking that it was the gardener, she said, "Sir, if thou have borne Him hence, tell me where thou hast laid Him, and I will take Him away." If this rich man's tomb was thought too honorable a burial place for Jesus, she herself would provide a place for Him. There was a grave that Christ's own voice had made vacant, the grave where Lazarus had lain. Might she not there find a burial place for her Lord? She felt that to care for His precious crucified body would be a great consolation to her in her grief.

But now in His own familiar voice Jesus said to her, "Mary." Now she knew that it was not a stranger who was addressing her, and turning she saw before her the living Christ. In her joy she forgot that He had been crucified. Springing toward Him, as if to embrace His feet, she said, "Rabboni." But Christ raised His hand, saying, Detain Me not; "for I am not yet ascended to My Father: but go to My brethren, and say unto them, I ascend unto My Father, and your Father; and to My God, and your God." And Mary went her way to the disciples with the joyful message.

Jesus refused to receive the homage of His people until He had the assurance that His sacrifice was accepted by the Father. He ascended to the heavenly courts, and from God Himself heard the assurance that His atonement for the sins of men had been ample, that through His blood all might gain eternal life. The Father ratified the covenant made with Christ, that He would receive repentant and obedient men, and would love them even as He loves His Son. Christ was to complete His work, and fulfill His pledge to "make a man more precious than fine gold; even a man than the golden wedge of Ophir." Isa. 13:12. All power in heaven and on earth was given to the Prince of Life, and He returned to His followers in a world of sin, that He might impart to them of His power and glory.

While the Saviour was in God's presence, receiving gifts for His church, the disciples thought upon His empty tomb, and mourned and wept. The day that was a day of rejoicing to all heaven was to the disciples a day of uncertainty, confusion, and perplexity. Their unbelief in the testimony of the women gives evidence of how low their faith had sunk. The news of Christ's resurrection was so different from what they had anticipated that they could not believe it. It was too good to be true, they thought. They had heard so much of the doctrines and the so-called scientific theories of the Sadducees that the impression made on their minds in regard to the resurrection was vague. They scarcely knew what the resurrection from the dead could mean. They were unable to take in the great subject.

"Go your way," the angels had said to the women, "tell His disciples and Peter that He goeth before you into Galilee: there shall ye see Him, as He said unto you." These angels had been with Christ as guardian angels throughout His life on earth. They had witnessed His trial and crucifixion. They had heard His words to His disciples. This was shown by their message to the disciples, and should have convinced them of its truth. Such words could have come only from the messengers of their risen Lord.

"Tell His disciples and Peter," the angels said. Since the death of Christ, Peter had been bowed down with remorse. His shameful denial of the Lord, and the Saviour's look of love and anguish, were ever before him. Of all the disciples he had suffered most bitterly. To him the assurance is given that his repentance is accepted and his sin forgiven. He is mentioned by name.

"Tell His disciples and Peter that He goeth before you into Galilee: there shall ye see Him." All the disciples had forsaken Jesus, and the call to meet Him again includes them all. He has not cast them off. When Mary Magdalene told them she had seen the Lord, she repeated the call to the meeting in Galilee. And a third time the message was sent to them. After He had ascended to the Father, Jesus appeared to the other women, saying, "All hail. And they came and held Him by the feet, and worshiped Him. Then said Jesus unto them, Be not afraid: go tell My brethren that they go into Galilee, and there shall they see Me."

Christ's first work on earth after His resurrection was to convince His disciples of His undiminished love and tender regard for them. To give them proof that He was their living Saviour, that He had broken the fetters of the tomb, and could no longer be held by the enemy death; to reveal that He had the same heart of love as when He was with them as their beloved Teacher, He appeared to them again and again. He would draw the bonds of love still closer around them. Go tell My brethren, He said, that they meet Me in Galilee.

As they heard this appointment, so definitely given, the disciples began to think of Christ's words to them foretelling His resurrection. But even now they did not rejoice. They could not cast off their doubt and perplexity. Even when the women declared that they had seen the Lord, the disciples would not believe. They thought them under an illusion.

Trouble seemed crowding upon trouble. On the sixth day of the week they had seen their Master die; on the first day of the next week they found themselves deprived of His body, and they were accused of having stolen it away for the sake of deceiving the people. They despaired of ever correcting the false impressions that were gaining ground against them. They feared the enmity of the priests and the wrath of the people. They longed for the presence of Jesus, who had helped them in every perplexity.

Often they repeated the words, "We trusted that it had been He which should have redeemed Israel." Lonely and sick at heart they remembered His words, "If they do these things in a green tree, what shall be done in the dry?" Luke 24:21; 23:31. They met together in the upper chamber, and closed and fastened the doors, knowing that the fate of their beloved Teacher might at any time be theirs.

And all the time they might have been rejoicing in the knowledge of a risen Saviour. In the garden, Mary had stood weeping, when Jesus was close beside her. Her eyes were so blinded by tears that she did not discern Him. And the hearts of the disciples were so full of grief that they did not believe the angels' message or the words of Christ Himself.

How many are still doing what these disciples did! How many echo Mary's despairing cry, "They have taken away the Lord, . . . and we know not where they have laid Him"! To how many might the Saviour's words be spoken, "Why weepest thou? whom seekest thou?" He is close beside them, but their tear-blinded eyes do not discern Him. He speaks to them, but they do not understand.

Oh that the bowed head might be lifted, that the eyes might be opened to behold Him, that the ears might listen to His voice! " Go quickly, and tell His disciples that He is risen." Bid them look not to Joseph's new tomb, that was closed with a great stone, and sealed with the Roman seal. Christ is not there. Look not to the empty sepulcher. Mourn not as those who are hopeless and helpless. Jesus lives, and because He lives, we shall live also. From grateful hearts, from lips touched with holy fire, let the glad song ring out, Christ is risen! He lives to make intercession for us. Grasp this hope, and it will hold the soul like a sure, tried anchor. Believe, and thou shalt see the glory of God

TEN

THE WALK TO EMMAUS

L ate in the afternoon of the day of the resurrection, two of the disciples were on their way to Emmaus, a little town eight miles from Jerusalem. These disciples had had no prominent place in Christ's work, but they were earnest believers in Him. They had come to the city to keep the Passover, and were greatly perplexed by the events that had recently taken place. They had heard the news of the morning in regard to the removal of Christ's body from the tomb, and also the report of the women who had seen the angels and had met Jesus. They were now returning to their homes to meditate and pray. Sadly they pursued their evening walk, talking over the scenes of the trial and the crucifixion. Never before had they been so utterly disheartened. Hopeless and faithless, they were walking in the shadow of the cross.

They had not advanced far on their journey when they were joined by a stranger, but they were so absorbed in their gloom and disappointment that they did not observe him closely. They continued their conversation, expressing the thoughts of their hearts. They were reasoning in regard to the lessons that Christ had given, which they seemed unable to comprehend. As they talked of the events that had taken place, Jesus longed to comfort them. He had seen their grief; He understood the conflicting, perplexing ideas that brought to their minds the thought, Can this Man, who suffered Himself to be so humiliated, be the Christ? Their grief could not be restrained, and they wept. Jesus knew that their hearts were bound up with Him in love, and He longed to wipe away their tears, and fill them with joy and gladness. But He must first give them lessons they would never forget.

"He said unto them, What manner of communications are these that ye have one to another, as ye walk, and are sad? And the one of them, whose name was Cleopas, answering said unto Him, Art Thou only a stranger in Jerusalem, and hast not known the things which are come to pass there in these days?" They told Him of their disappointment in regard to their Master, "which was a prophet mighty in deed and word before God and all the people;" but "the chief priests and our rulers," they said, "delivered Him to be condemned to death, and have crucified Him." With hearts sore with disappointment, and with quivering lips, they added, "We trusted that it had been He which should have redeemed Israel: and beside all this, today is the third day since these things were done."

Strange that the disciples did not remember Christ's words, and realize that He had foretold the events which had come to pass! They did not realize that the last part of His disclosure would be just as verily fulfilled as the first part, that the third day He would rise again. This was the part they should have remembered. The priests and rulers did not forget this. On the day "that followed the day of the preparation, the chief priests and Pharisees came together unto Pilate, saying, Sir, we remember that that deceiver said, while He was yet alive, After three days I will rise again." Matt. 27:62, 63. But the disciples did not remember these words.

"Then He said unto them, O fools, and slow of heart to believe all that the prophets have spoken: ought not Christ to have suffered these things, and to enter into His glory?" The disciples wondered who this stranger could be, that He should penetrate to their very souls, and speak with such earnestness, tenderness, and sympathy, and with such hopefulness. For the first time since Christ's betrayal, they began to feel hopeful. Often they looked earnestly at their companion, and thought that His words were just the words that Christ would have spoken. They were filled with amazement, and their hearts began to throb with joyful expectation.

Beginning at Moses, the very Alpha of Bible history, Christ expounded in all the Scriptures the things concerning Himself. Had

He first made Himself known to them, their hearts would have been satisfied. In the fullness of their joy they would have hungered for nothing more. But it was necessary for them to understand the witness borne to Him by the types and prophecies of the Old Testament. Upon these their faith must be established. Christ performed no miracle to convince them, but it was His first work to explain the Scriptures. They had looked upon His death as the destruction of all their hopes. Now He showed from the prophets that this was the very strongest evidence for their faith.

In teaching these disciples, Jesus showed the importance of the Old Testament as a witness to His mission. Many professed Christians now discard the Old Testament, claiming that it is no longer of any use. But such is not Christ's teaching. So highly did He value it that at one time He said, "If they hear not Moses and the prophets, neither will they be persuaded, though one rose from the dead." Luke 16:31.

It is the voice of Christ that speaks through patriarchs and prophets, from the days of Adam even to the closing scenes of time. The Saviour is revealed in the Old Testament as clearly as in the New. It is the light from the prophetic past that brings out the life of Christ and the teachings of the New Testament with clearness and beauty. The miracles of Christ are a proof of His divinity; but a stronger proof that He is the world's Redeemer is found in comparing the prophecies of the Old Testament with the history of the New.

Reasoning from prophecy, Christ gave His disciples a correct idea of what He was to be in humanity. Their expectation of a Messiah who was to take His throne and kingly power in accordance with the desires of men had been misleading. It would interfere with a correct apprehension of His descent from the highest to the lowest position that could be occupied. Christ desired that the ideas of His disciples might be pure and true in every specification. They must understand as far as possible in regard to the cup of suffering that had been apportioned to Him. He showed them that the awful conflict which they could not yet comprehend was the fulfillment of the covenant made before the foundation of the world was laid. Christ must die, as every transgressor of the law must die if he continues in sin. All this was to be, but it was not to end in defeat, but in glorious, eternal victory. Jesus told them that every effort must be made to save the world from sin. His followers must live as He lived, and work as He worked, with intense, persevering effort.

Thus Christ discoursed to His disciples, opening their minds that they might understand the Scriptures. The disciples were weary, but the conversation did not flag. Words of life and assurance fell from the Saviour's lips. But still their eyes were holden. As He told them of the overthrow of Jerusalem, they looked upon the doomed city with weeping. But little did they yet suspect who their traveling companion was. They did not think that the subject of their conversation was walking by their side; for Christ referred to Himself as though He were another person. They thought that He was one of those who had been in attendance at the great feast, and who was now returning to his home. He walked as carefully as they over the rough stones, now and then halting with them for a little rest. Thus they proceeded along the mountainous road, while the One who was soon to take His position at God's right hand, and who could say, "All power is given unto Me in heaven and in earth," walked beside them. Matt. 28:18.

During the journey the sun had gone down, and before the travelers reached their place of rest, the laborers in the fields had left their work. As the disciples were about to enter their home, the stranger appeared as though He would continue His journey. But the disciples felt drawn to Him. Their souls hungered to hear more from Him. "Abide with us," they said. He did not seem to accept the invitation, but they pressed it upon Him, urging, "It is toward evening, and the day is far spent." Christ yielded to this entreaty and "went in to tarry with them."

Had the disciples failed to press their invitation, they would not have known that their traveling companion was the risen Lord. Christ never forces His company upon anyone. He interests Himself in those who need Him. Gladly will He enter the humblest home, and cheer the lowliest heart. But if men are too indifferent to think of the heavenly Guest, or ask Him to abide with them, He passes on. Thus many meet with great loss. They do not know Christ any more than did the disciples as He walked with them by the way.

The simple evening meal of bread is soon prepared. It is placed before the guest, who has taken His seat at the head of the table. Now He puts forth His hands to bless the food. The disciples start back in astonishment. Their companion spreads forth His hands in exactly the same way as their Master used to do. They look again, and lo, they see in His hands the print of nails. Both exclaim at once, It is the Lord Jesus! He has risen from the dead!

They rise to cast themselves at His feet and worship Him, but He has vanished out of their sight. They look at the place which had been occupied by One whose body had lately lain in the grave, and say to each other, "Did not our heart burn within us, while He talked with us by the way, and while He opened to us the Scriptures?"

But with this great news to communicate they cannot sit and talk. Their weariness and hunger are gone. They leave their meal untasted, and full of joy immediately set out again on the same path by which they came, hurrying to tell the tidings to the disciples in the city. In some parts the road is not safe, but they climb over the steep places, slipping on the smooth rocks. They do not see, they do not know, that they have the protection of Him who has traveled the road with them. With their pilgrim staff in hand, they press on, desiring to go faster than they dare. They lose their track, but find it again. Sometimes running, sometimes stumbling, they press forward, their unseen Companion close beside them all the way.

The night is dark, but the Sun of Righteousness is shining upon them. Their hearts leap for joy. They seem to be in a new world. Christ is a living Saviour. They no longer mourn over Him as dead. Christ is risen—over and over again they repeat it. This is the message they are carrying to the sorrowing ones. They must tell them the wonderful story of the walk to Emmaus. They must tell who joined them by the way. They carry the greatest message ever given to the world, a message of glad tidings upon which the hopes of the human family for time and for eternity depend.

ELEVEN

"PEACE BE UNTO YOU"

O n reaching Jerusalem the two disciples enter at the eastern gate, which is open at night on festal occasions. The houses are dark and silent, but the travelers make their way through the narrow streets by the light of the rising moon. They go to the upper chamber where Jesus spent the hours of the last evening before His death. Here they know that their brethren are to be found. Late as it is, they know that the disciples will not sleep till they learn for a certainty what has become of the body of their Lord. They find the door of the chamber securely barred. They knock for admission, but no answer comes. All is still. Then they give their names. The door is carefully unbarred, they enter, and Another, unseen, enters with them. Then the door is again fastened, to keep out spies.

The travelers find all in surprised excitement. The voices of those in the room break out into thanksgiving and praise, saying, "The Lord is risen indeed, and hath appeared to Simon." Then the two travelers, panting with the haste with which they have made their journey, tell the wondrous story of how Jesus has appeared to them. They have just ended, and some are saying that they cannot believe it, for it is too good to be true, when behold, another Person stands before them. Every eye is fastened upon the stranger. No one has knocked for entrance. No footstep has been heard. The disciples are startled, and wonder what it means. Then they hear a voice which is no other than the voice of their Master. Clear and distinct the words fall from His lips, "Peace be unto you."

"But they were terrified and affrighted, and supposed that they had seen a spirit. And He said unto them, Why are ye troubled? and why do thoughts arise in your hearts? Behold My hands and My feet, that it is I Myself: handle Me, and see; for a spirit hath not flesh and bones, as ye see Me have. And when He had thus spoken, He showed them His hands and His feet."

They beheld the hands and feet marred by the cruel nails. They recognized His voice, like no other they had ever heard. "And while they yet believed not for joy, and wondered, He said unto them, Have ye here any meat? And they gave Him a piece of a broiled fish, and of an honeycomb. And He took it, and did eat before them." "Then were the disciples glad, when they saw the Lord." Faith and joy took the place of unbelief, and with feelings which no words could express they acknowledged their risen Saviour.

At the birth of Jesus the angel announced, Peace on earth, and good will to men. And now at His first appearance to the disciples after His resurrection, the Saviour addressed them with the blessed words, "Peace be unto you." Jesus is ever ready to speak peace to souls that are burdened with doubts and fears. He waits for us to open the door of the heart to Him, and say, Abide with us. He says, "Behold, I stand at the door, and knock: if any man hear My voice, and open the door, I will come in to him, and will sup with him, and he with Me." Rev. 3:20.

The resurrection of Jesus was a type of the final resurrection of all who sleep in Him. The countenance of the risen Saviour, His manner, His speech, were all familiar to His disciples. As Jesus arose from the dead, so those who sleep in Him are to rise again. We shall know our friends, even as the disciples knew Jesus. They may have been deformed, diseased, or disfigured, in this mortal life, and they rise in perfect health and symmetry; yet in the glorified body their identity will be perfectly preserved. Then shall we know even as also we are known. 1 Cor. 13:12. In the face radiant with the light shining from the face of Jesus, we shall recognize the lineaments of those we love.

When Jesus met with His disciples, He reminded them of the words He had spoken to them before His death, that all things must be fulfilled which were written in the law of Moses, and in the prophets, and in the Psalms concerning Him. "Then opened He their understanding, that they might understand the Scriptures, and said unto them, Thus it is written, and thus it behooved Christ to suffer, and to rise from the dead the third day: and that repentance and remission of sins should be preached in His name among all nations, beginning at Jerusalem. And ye are witnesses of these things."

The disciples began to realize the nature and extent of their work. They were to proclaim to the world the wonderful truths which Christ had entrusted to them. The events of His life, His death and resurrection, the prophecies that pointed to these events, the sacredness of the law of God, the mysteries of the plan of salvation, the power of Jesus for the remission of sins,—to all these things they were witnesses, and they were to make them known to the world. They were to proclaim the gospel of peace and salvation through repentance and the power of the Saviour.

"And when He had said this, He breathed on them, and saith unto them, Receive ye the Holy Ghost: Whosoever sins ye remit, they are remitted unto them; and whosoever sins ye retain, they are retained." The Holy Spirit was not yet fully manifested; for Christ had not yet been glorified. The more abundant impartation of the Spirit did not take place till after Christ's ascension. Not until this was received could the disciples fulfill the commission to preach the gospel to the world. But the Spirit was now given for a special purpose. Before the disciples could fulfill their official duties in connection with the church, Christ breathed His Spirit upon them. He was committing to them a most sacred trust, and He desired to impress them with the fact that without the Holy Spirit this work could not be accomplished.

The Holy Spirit is the breath of spiritual life in the soul. The impartation of the Spirit is the impartation of the life of Christ. It imbues the receiver with the attributes of Christ. Only those who are thus taught of God, those who possess the inward working of the Spirit, and in whose life the Christ-life is manifested, are to stand as representative men, to minister in behalf of the church.

"Whosoever sins ye remit," said Christ, "they are remitted; . . .

and whosesoever sins ye retain, they are retained." Christ here gives no liberty for any man to pass judgment upon others. In the Sermon on the Mount He forbade this. It is the prerogative of God. But on the church in its organized capacity He places a responsibility for the individual members. Toward those who fall into sin, the church has a duty, to warn, to instruct, and if possible to restore. "Reprove, rebuke, exhort," the Lord says, "with all long-suffering and doctrine." 2 Tim. 4:2. Deal faithfully with wrongdoing. Warn every soul that is in danger. Leave none to deceive themselves. Call sin by its right name. Declare what God has said in regard to lying, Sabbathbreaking, stealing, idolatry, and every other evil. "They which do such things shall not inherit the kingdom of God." Gal. 5:21. If they persist in sin, the judgment you have declared from God's word is pronounced upon them in heaven. In choosing to sin, they disown Christ; the church must show that she does not sanction their deeds, or she herself dishonors her Lord. She must say about sin what God says about it. She must deal with it as God directs, and her action is ratified in heaven. He who despises the authority of the church despises the authority of Christ Himself.

But there is a brighter side to the picture. "Whosesoever sins ye remit, they are remitted." Let this thought be kept uppermost. In labor for the erring, let every eye be directed to Christ. Let the shepherds have a tender care for the flock of the Lord's pasture. Let them speak to the erring of the forgiving mercy of the Saviour. Let them encourage the sinner to repent, and believe in Him who can pardon. Let them declare, on the authority of God's word, "If we confess our sins, He is faithful and just to forgive us our sins, and to cleanse us from all unrighteousness." 1 John 1:9. All who repent have the assurance, "He will have compassion upon us; He will subdue our iniquities; and Thou wilt cast all their sins into the depths of the sea." Micah 7:19.

Let the repentance of the sinner be accepted by the church with grateful hearts. Let the repenting one be led out from the darkness of unbelief into the light of faith and righteousness. Let his trembling hand be placed in the loving hand of Jesus. Such a remission is ratified in heaven.

Only in this sense has the church power to absolve the sinner. Remission of sins can be obtained only through the merits of Christ. To no man, to no body of men, is given power to free the soul from guilt. Christ charged His disciples to preach the remission of sins in His name among all nations; but they themselves were not empowered to remove one stain of sin. The name of Jesus is the only "name under heaven given among men, whereby we must be saved." Acts 4:12.

When Jesus first met the disciples in the upper chamber, Thomas was not with them. He heard the reports of the others, and received abundant proof that Jesus had risen; but gloom and unbelief filled his heart. As he heard the disciples tell of the wonderful manifestations of the risen Saviour, it only plunged him in deeper despair. If Jesus had really risen from the dead, there could be no further hope of a literal earthly kingdom. And it wounded his vanity to think that his Master should reveal Himself to all the disciples except him. He was determined not to believe, and for a whole week he brooded over his wretchedness, which seemed all the darker in contrast with the hope and faith of his brethren.

During this time he repeatedly declared, "Except I shall see in His hands the print of the nails, and put my finger into the print of the nails, and thrust my hand into His side, I will not believe." He would not see through the eyes of his brethren, or exercise faith which was dependent upon their testimony. He ardently loved his Lord, but he had allowed jealousy and unbelief to take possession of his mind and heart.

A number of the disciples now made the familiar upper chamber their temporary home, and at evening all except Thomas gathered here. One evening Thomas determined to meet with the others. Notwithstanding his unbelief, he had a faint hope that the good news was true. While the disciples were taking their evening meal, they talked of the evidences which Christ had given them in the prophecies. "Then came Jesus, the doors being shut, and stood in the midst, and said, Peace be unto you."

Turning to Thomas He said, "Reach hither thy finger, and behold My hands; and reach hither thy hand, and thrust it into My side: and be not faithless, but believing." These words showed that He was acquainted with the thoughts and words of Thomas. The doubting disciple knew that none of his companions had seen Jesus for a week. They could not have told the Master of his unbelief. He recognized the One before him as his Lord. He had no desire for further proof. His heart leaped for joy, and he cast himself at the feet of Jesus crying, "My Lord and my God."

Jesus accepted his acknowledgment, but gently reproved his unbelief: "Thomas, because thou hast seen Me, thou hast believed: blessed are they that have not seen, and yet have believed." The faith of Thomas would have been more pleasing to Christ if he had been willing to believe upon the testimony of his brethren. Should the world now follow the example of Thomas, no one would believe unto salvation; for all who receive Christ must do so through the testimony of others.

Many who are given to doubt excuse themselves by saying that if they had the evidence which Thomas had from his companions, they would believe. They do not realize that they have not only that evidence, but much more. Many who, like Thomas, wait for all cause of doubt to be removed, will never realize their desire. They gradually become confirmed in unbelief. Those who educate themselves to look on the dark side, and murmur and complain, know not what they do. They are sowing the seeds of doubt, and they will have a harvest of doubt to reap. At a time when faith and confidence are most essential, many will thus find themselves powerless to hope and believe.

In His treatment of Thomas, Jesus gave a lesson for His followers. His example shows how we should treat those whose faith is weak, and who make their doubts prominent. Jesus did not overwhelm Thomas with reproach, nor did He enter into controversy with him. He revealed Himself to the doubting one. Thomas had been most unreasonable in dictating the conditions of his faith, but Jesus, by His generous love and consideration, broke down all the barriers. Unbelief is seldom overcome by controversy. It is rather put upon self-defense, and finds new support and excuse. But let Jesus, in His love and mercy, be revealed as the crucified Saviour, and from many once unwilling lips will be heard the acknowledgment of Thomas, "My Lord and my God."

TWELVE

BY THE SEA ONCE MORE

Jesus had appointed to meet His disciples in Galilee; and soon after the Passover week was ended, they bent their steps thither. Their absence from Jerusalem during the feast would have been interpreted as disaffection and heresy, therefore they remained till its close; but this over, they gladly turned homeward to meet the Saviour as He had directed.

Seven of the disciples were in company. They were clad in the humble garb of fishermen; they were poor in worldly goods, but rich in the knowledge and practice of the truth, which in the sight of Heaven gave them the highest rank as teachers. They had not been students in the schools of the prophets, but for three years they had been taught by the greatest Educator the world has ever known. Under His instruction they had become elevated, intelligent, and refined, agents through whom men might be led to a knowledge of the truth.

Much of the time of Christ's ministry had been passed near the Sea of Galilee. As the disciples gathered in a place where they were not likely to be disturbed, they found themselves surrounded by reminders of Jesus and His mighty works. On this sea, when their hearts were filled with terror, and the fierce storm was hurrying them to destruction, Jesus had walked upon the billows to their rescue. Here the tempest had been hushed by His word. Within sight was the beach where above ten thousand persons had been fed from a few small loaves and fishes. Not far distant was Capernaum, the scene of so many miracles. As the disciples looked upon the scene, their minds were full of the words and deeds of their Saviour.

The evening was pleasant, and Peter, who still had much of his old love for boats and fishing, proposed that they should go out upon the sea and cast their nets. In this plan all were ready to join; they were in need of food and clothing, which the proceeds of a successful night's fishing would supply. So they went out in their boat, but they caught nothing. All night they toiled, without success. Through the weary hours they talked of their absent Lord, and recalled the wonderful events they had witnessed in His ministry beside the sea. They questioned as to their own future, and grew sad at the prospect before them.

All the while a lone watcher upon the shore followed them with His eye, while He Himself was unseen. At length the morning dawned. The boat was but a little way from the shore, and the disciples saw a stranger standing upon the beach, who accosted them with the question, "Children, have ye any meat?" When they answered, "No," "He said unto them, Cast the net on the right side of the ship, and ye shall find. They cast therefore, and now they were not able to draw it for the multitude of fishes."

John recognized the stranger, and exclaimed to Peter, "It is the Lord." Peter was so elated and so glad that in his eagerness he cast himself into the water and was soon standing by the side of his Master. The other disciples came in their boat, dragging the net with fishes. "As soon then as they were come to land, they saw a fire of coals there, and fish laid thereon, and bread."

They were too much amazed to question whence came the fire and the food. "Jesus saith unto them, Bring of the fish which ye have now caught." Peter rushed for the net, which he had dropped, and helped his brethren drag it to the shore. After the work was done, and the preparation made, Jesus bade the disciples come and dine. He broke the food, and divided it among them, and was known and acknowledged by all the seven. The miracle of feeding the five thousand on the mountainside was now brought to their minds; but a mysterious awe was upon them, and in silence they gazed upon the risen Saviour.

Vividly they recalled the scene beside the sea when Jesus had bidden them follow Him. They remembered how, at His command, they had launched out into the deep, and had let down their net, and the catch had been so abundant as to fill the net, even to breaking. Then Jesus had called them to leave their fishing boats, and had promised to make them fishers of men. It was to bring this scene to their minds, and to deepen its impression, that He had again performed the miracle. His act was a renewal of the commission to the disciples. It showed them that the death of their Master had not lessened their obligation to do the work He had assigned them. Though they were to be deprived of His personal companionship, and of the means of support by their former employment, the risen Saviour would still have a care for them. While they were doing His work, He would provide for their needs. And Jesus had a purpose in bidding them cast their net on the right side of the ship. On that side He stood upon the shore. That was the side of faith. If they labored in connection with Him,—His divine power combining with their human effort,—they could not fail of success.

Another lesson Christ had to give, relating especially to Peter. Peter's denial of his Lord had been in shameful contrast to his former professions of loyalty. He had dishonored Christ, and had incurred the distrust of his brethren. They thought he would not be allowed to take his former position among them, and he himself felt that he had forfeited his trust. Before being called to take up again his apostolic work, he must before them all give evidence of his repentance. Without this, his sin, though repented of, might have destroyed his influence as a minister of Christ. The Saviour gave him opportunity to regain the confidence of his brethren, and, so far as possible, to remove the reproach he had brought upon the gospel.

Here is given a lesson for all Christ's followers. The gospel makes no compromise with evil. It cannot excuse sin. Secret sins are to be confessed in secret to God; but, for open sin, open confession is required. The reproach of the disciple's sin is cast upon Christ. It causes Satan to triumph, and wavering souls to stumble. By giving proof of repentance, the disciple, so far as lies in his power, is to remove this reproach.

While Christ and the disciples were eating together by the seaside, the Saviour said to Peter, "Simon, son of Jonas, lovest thou Me more than these?" referring to his brethren. Peter had once declared, "Though all men shall be offended because of Thee, yet will I never be offended." Matt. 26:33. But he now put a truer estimate upon himself. "Yea, Lord," he said, "Thou knowest that I love Thee." There is no vehement assurance that his love is greater than that of his brethren. He does not express his own opinion of his devotion. To Him who can read all the motives of the heart he appeals to judge as to his sincerity,—"Thou knowest that I love Thee." And Jesus bids him, "Feed My lambs."

Again Jesus applied the test to Peter, repeating His former words: "Simon, son of Jonas, lovest thou Me?" This time He did not ask Peter whether he loved Him better than did his brethren. The second response was like the first, free from extravagant assurance: "Yea, Lord; Thou knowest that I love Thee." Jesus said to him, "Feed My sheep." Once more the Saviour put the trying question: "Simon, son of Jonas, lovest thou Me?" Peter was grieved; he thought that Jesus doubted his love. He knew that his Lord had cause to distrust him, and with an aching heart he answered, "Lord, Thou knowest all things; Thou knowest that I love Thee." Again Jesus said to him, "Feed My sheep."

Three times Peter had openly denied his Lord, and three times Jesus drew from him the assurance of his love and loyalty, pressing home that pointed question, like a barbed arrow to his wounded heart. Before the assembled disciples Jesus revealed the depth of Peter's repentance, and showed how thoroughly humbled was the once boasting disciple.

Peter was naturally forward and impulsive, and Satan had taken advantage of these characteristics to overthrow him. Just before the fall of Peter, Jesus had said to him, "Satan hath desired to have you, that he may sift you as wheat: but I have prayed for thee, that thy faith fail not: and when thou art converted, strengthen thy brethren." Luke 22:31, 32. That time had now come, and the transformation in Peter was evident. The close, testing questions of the Lord had not called out one forward, self-sufficient reply; and because of his humiliation and repentance, Peter was better prepared than ever before to act as shepherd to the flock.

The first work that Christ entrusted to Peter on restoring him to the ministry was to feed the lambs. This was a work in which Peter had little experience. It would require great care and tenderness, much patience and perseverance. It called him to minister to those who were young in the faith, to teach the ignorant, to open the Scriptures to them, and to educate them for usefulness in Christ's service. Heretofore Peter had not been fitted to do this, or even to understand its importance. But this was the work which Jesus now called upon him to do. For this work his own experience of suffering and repentance had prepared him.

Before his fall, Peter was always speaking unadvisedly, from the impulse of the moment. He was always ready to correct others, and to express his mind, before he had a clear comprehension of himself or of what he had to say. But the converted Peter was very different. He retained his former fervor, but the grace of Christ regulated his zeal. He was no longer impetuous, self-confident, and self-exalted, but calm, self-possessed, and teachable. He could then feed the lambs as well as the sheep of Christ's flock.

The Saviour's manner of dealing with Peter had a lesson for him and for his brethren. It taught them to meet the transgressor with patience, sympathy, and forgiving love. Although Peter had denied his Lord, the love which Jesus bore him never faltered. Just such love should the undershepherd feel for the sheep and lambs committed to his care. Remembering his own weakness and failure, Peter was to deal with his flock as tenderly as Christ had dealt with him.

The question that Christ had put to Peter was significant. He mentioned only one condition of discipleship and service. "Lovest thou Me?" He said. This is the essential qualification. Though Peter might possess every other, yet without the love of Christ he could not be a faithful shepherd over the Lord's flock. Knowledge, benevolence, eloquence, gratitude, and zeal are all aids in the good work; but without the love of Jesus in the heart, the work of the Christian minister is a failure.

Jesus walked alone with Peter, for there was something which He wished to communicate to him only. Before His death, Jesus had said to him, "Whither I go, thou canst not follow Me now; but thou shalt follow Me afterwards." To this Peter had replied, "Lord, why cannot I follow Thee now? I will lay down my life for Thy sake." John 13:36, 37. When he said this, he little knew to what heights and depths Christ's feet would lead the way. Peter had failed when the test came, but again he was to have opportunity to prove his love for Christ. That he might be strengthened for the final test of his faith, the Saviour opened to him his future. He told him that after living a life of usefulness, when age was telling upon his strength, he would indeed follow his Lord. Jesus said, "When thou wast young, thou girdedst thyself, and walkedst whither thou wouldest: but when thou shalt be old, thou shalt stretch forth thy hands, and another shall gird thee, and carry thee whither thou wouldest not. This spake He, signifying by what death he should glorify God."

Jesus thus made known to Peter the very manner of his death; He even foretold the stretching forth of his hands upon the cross. Again He bade His disciple, "Follow Me." Peter was not disheartened by the revelation. He felt willing to suffer any death for his Lord.

Heretofore Peter had known Christ after the flesh, as many know Him now; but he was no more to be thus limited. He knew Him no more as he had known Him in his association with Him in humanity. He had loved Him as a man, as a heaven-sent teacher; he now loved Him as God. He had been learning the lesson that to him Christ was all in all. Now he was prepared to share in his Lord's mission of sacrifice. When at last brought to the cross, he was, at his own request, crucified with his head downward. He thought it too great an honor to suffer in the same way as his Master did.

To Peter the words "Follow Me" were full of instruction. Not only for his death, but for every step of his life, was the lesson given.

Hitherto Peter had been inclined to act independently. He had tried to plan for the work of God, instead of waiting to follow out God's plan. But he could gain nothing by rushing on before the Lord. Jesus bids him, "Follow Me." Do not run ahead of Me. Then you will not have the hosts of Satan to meet alone. Let Me go before you, and you will not be overcome by the enemy.

As Peter walked beside Jesus, he saw that John was following. A desire came over him to know his future, and he "saith to Jesus, Lord, and what shall this man do? Jesus saith unto him, If I will that he tarry till I come, what is that to thee? follow thou Me." Peter should have considered that his Lord would reveal to him all that it was best for him to know. It is the duty of everyone to follow Christ, without undue anxiety as to the work assigned to others. In saying of John, "If I will that he tarry till I come," Jesus gave no assurance that this disciple should live until the Lord's second coming. He merely asserted His own supreme power, and that even if He should will this to be so, it would in no way affect Peter's work. The future of both John and Peter was in the hands of their Lord. Obedience in following Him was the duty required of each.

How many today are like Peter! They are interested in the affairs of others, and anxious to know their duty, while they are in danger of neglecting their own. It is our work to look to Christ and follow Him. We shall see mistakes in the lives of others, and defects in their character. Humanity is encompassed with infirmity. But in Christ we shall find perfection. Beholding Him, we shall become transformed.

John lived to be very aged. He witnessed the destruction of Jerusalem, and the ruin of the stately temple,—a symbol of the final ruin of the world. To his latest days John closely followed his Lord. The burden of his testimony to the churches was, "Beloved, let us love one another;" "he that dwelleth in love, dwelleth in God, and God in him." 1 John 4:7, 16.

Peter had been restored to his apostleship, but the honor and authority he received from Christ had not given him supremacy over his brethren. This Christ had made plain when in answer to Peter's question, "What shall this man do?" He had said, "What is that to thee? follow thou Me." Peter was not honored as the head of the church. The favor which Christ had shown him in forgiving his apostasy, and entrusting him with the feeding of the flock, and Peter's own faithfulness in following Christ, won for him the confidence of his brethren. He had much influence in the church. But the lesson which Christ had taught him by the Sea of Galilee Peter carried with him throughout his life. Writing by the Holy Spirit to the churches, he said:

"The elders which are among you I exhort, who am also an elder, and a witness of the sufferings of Christ, and also a partaker of the glory that shall be revealed: Feed the flock of God which is among you, taking the oversight thereof, not by constraint, but willingly; not for filthy lucre, but of a ready mind; neither as being lords over God's heritage, but being ensamples to the flock. And when the Chief Shepherd shall appear, ye shall receive a crown of glory that fadeth not away." 1 Peter 5:1-4.

THIRTEEN

GO TEACH ALL NATIONS

Standing but a step from His heavenly throne, Christ gave the commission to His disciples. "All power is given unto Me in heaven and in earth," He said. "Go ye therefore, and teach all nations." "Go ye into all the world, and preach the gospel to every creature." Mark 16:15. Again and again the words were repeated, that the disciples might grasp their significance. Upon all the inhabitants of the earth, high and low, rich and poor, was the light of heaven to shine in clear, strong rays. The disciples were to be colaborers with their Redeemer in the work of saving the world.

The commission had been given to the twelve when Christ met with them in the upper chamber; but it was now to be given to a larger number. At the meeting on a mountain in Galilee, all the believers who could be called together were assembled. Of this meeting Christ Himself, before His death, had designated the time and place. The angel at the tomb reminded the disciples of His promise to meet them in Galilee. The promise was repeated to the believers who were gathered at Jerusalem during the Passover week, and through them it reached many lonely ones who were mourning the death of their Lord. With intense interest all looked forward to the interview. They made their way to the place of meeting by circuitous routes, coming in from every direction, to avoid exciting the suspicion of the jealous Jews. With wondering hearts they came, talking earnestly together of the news that had reached them concerning Christ.

At the time appointed, about five hundred believers were collected in little knots on the mountainside, eager to learn all that could be learned from those who had seen Christ since His resurrection. From group to group the disciples passed, telling all they had seen and

heard of Jesus, and reasoning from the Scriptures as He had done with them. Thomas recounted the story of his unbelief, and told how his doubts had been swept away. Suddenly Jesus stood among them. No one could tell whence or how He came. Many who were present had never before seen Him; but in His hands and feet they beheld the marks of the crucifixion; His countenance was as the face of God, and when they saw Him, they worshiped Him.

But some doubted. So it will always be. There are those who find it hard to exercise faith, and they place themselves on the doubting side. These lose much because of their unbelief.

This was the only interview that Jesus had with many of the believers after His resurrection. He came and spoke to them saying, "All power is given unto Me in heaven and in earth." The disciples had worshiped Him before He spoke, but His words, falling from lips that had been closed in death, thrilled them with peculiar power. He was now the risen Saviour. Many of them had seen Him exercise His power in healing the sick and controlling satanic agencies. They believed that He possessed power to set up His kingdom at Jerusalem, power to quell all opposition, power over the elements of nature. He had stilled the angry waters; He had walked upon the white-crested billows; He had raised the dead to life. Now He declared that "all power" was given to Him. His words carried the minds of His hearers above earthly and temporal things to the heavenly and eternal. They were lifted to the highest conception of His dignity and glory.

Christ's words on the mountainside were the announcement that His sacrifice in behalf of man was full and complete. The conditions of the atonement had been fulfilled; the work for which He came to this world had been accomplished. He was on His way to the throne of God, to be honored by angels, principalities, and powers. He had entered upon His mediatorial work. Clothed with boundless authority, He gave His commission to the disciples: "Go ye therefore, and teach all nations," "baptizing them into the name of the Father and of the Son and of the Holy Spirit: teaching them to observe all things whatsoever I commanded you: and lo, I am with you always, even

unto the end of the world." Matt. 28:19, 20, R. V.

The Jewish people had been made the depositaries of sacred truth; but Pharisaism had made them the most exclusive, the most bigoted, of all the human race. Everything about the priests and rulers—their dress, customs, ceremonies, traditions—made them unfit to be the light of the world. They looked upon themselves, the Jewish nation, as the world. But Christ commissioned His disciples to proclaim a faith and worship that would have in it nothing of caste or country, a faith that would be adapted to all peoples, all nations, all classes of men.

Before leaving His disciples, Christ plainly stated the nature of His kingdom. He called to their minds what He had previously told them concerning it. He declared that it was not His purpose to establish in this world a temporal, but a spiritual kingdom. He was not to reign as an earthly king on David's throne. Again He opened to them the Scriptures, showing that all He had passed through had been ordained in heaven, in the councils between the Father and Himself. All had been foretold by men inspired by the Holy Spirit. He said, You see that all I have revealed to you concerning My rejection as the Messiah has come to pass. All I have said in regard to the humiliation I should endure and the death I should die, has been verified. On the third day I rose again. Search the Scriptures more diligently, and you will see that in all these things the specifications of prophecy concerning Me have been fulfilled.

Christ commissioned His disciples to do the work He had left in their hands, beginning at Jerusalem. Jerusalem had been the scene of His amazing condescension for the human race. There He had suffered, been rejected and condemned. The land of Judea was His birthplace. There, clad in the garb of humanity, He had walked with men, and few had discerned how near heaven came to the earth when Jesus was among them. At Jerusalem the work of the disciples must begin.

In view of all that Christ had suffered there, and the unappreciated labor He had put forth, the disciples might have pleaded for a more promising field; but they made no such plea. The very ground where He had scattered the seed of truth was to be cultivated by the disciples, and the seed would spring up and yield an abundant harvest. In their work the disciples would have to meet persecution through the jealousy and hatred of the Jews; but this had been endured by their Master, and they were not to flee from it. The first offers of mercy must be made to the murderers of the Saviour.

And there were in Jerusalem many who had secretly believed on Jesus, and many who had been deceived by the priests and rulers. To these also the gospel was to be presented. They were to be called to repentance. The wonderful truth that through Christ alone could remission of sins be obtained was to be made plain. While all Jerusalem was stirred by the thrilling events of the past few weeks, the preaching of the gospel would make the deepest impression.

But the work was not to stop here. It was to be extended to the earth's remotest bounds. To His disciples Christ said, You have been witnesses of My life of self-sacrifice in behalf of the world. You have witnessed My labors for Israel. Although they would not come unto Me that they might have life, although priests and rulers have done to Me as they listed, although they have rejected Me as the Scriptures foretold, they shall have still another opportunity of accepting the Son of God. You have seen that all who come to Me, confessing their sins, I freely receive. Him that cometh to Me I will in nowise cast out. All who will, may be reconciled to God, and receive everlasting life. To you, My disciples, I commit this message of mercy. It is to be given to Israel first, and then to all nations, tongues, and peoples. It is to be given to Jews and Gentiles. All who believe are to be gathered into one church.

Through the gift of the Holy Spirit the disciples were to receive a marvelous power. Their testimony was to be confirmed by signs and wonders. Miracles would be wrought, not only by the apostles, but by those who received their message. Jesus said, "In My name shall they cast out devils; they shall speak with new tongues; they shall take up serpents; and if they drink any deadly thing, it shall not hurt them; they shall lay hands on the sick, and they shall recover." Mark 16:17, 18.

At that time poisoning was often practiced. Unscrupulous men did not hesitate to remove by this means those who stood in the way of their ambition. Jesus knew that the life of His disciples would thus be imperiled. Many would think it doing God service to put His witnesses to death. He therefore promised them protection from this danger.

The disciples were to have the same power which Jesus had to heal "all manner of sickness and all manner of disease among the people." By healing in His name the diseases of the body, they would testify to His power for the healing of the soul. Matt. 4:23; 9:6. And a new endowment was now promised. The disciples were to preach among other nations, and they would receive power to speak other tongues. The apostles and their associates were unlettered men, yet through the outpouring of the Spirit on the day of Pentecost, their speech, whether in their own or a foreign language, became pure, simple, and accurate, both in word and in accent.

Thus Christ gave His disciples their commission. He made full provision for the prosecution of the work, and took upon Himself the responsibility for its success. So long as they obeyed His word, and worked in connection with Him, they could not fail. Go to all nations, He bade them. Go to the farthest part of the habitable globe, but know that My presence will be there. Labor in faith and confidence, for the time will never come when I will forsake you.

The Saviour's commission to the disciples included all the believers. It includes all believers in Christ to the end of time. It is a fatal mistake to suppose that the work of saving souls depends alone on the ordained minister. All to whom the heavenly inspiration has come are put in trust with the gospel. All who receive the life of Christ are ordained to work for the salvation of their fellow men. For this work the church was established, and all who take upon themselves its sacred vows are thereby pledged to be co-workers with Christ.

"The Spirit and the bride say, Come. And let him that heareth say, Come." Rev. 22:17. Everyone who hears is to repeat the invitation. Whatever one's calling in life, his first interest should be to win souls for Christ. He may not be able to speak to congregations, but he can work for individuals. To them he can communicate the instruction received from his Lord. Ministry does not consist alone in preaching. Those minister who relieve the sick and suffering, helping the needy, speaking words of comfort to the desponding and those of little faith. Nigh and afar off are souls weighed down by a sense of guilt. It is not hardship, toil, or poverty that degrades humanity. It is guilt, wrong-doing. This brings unrest and dissatisfaction. Christ would have His servants minister to sin-sick souls.

The disciples were to begin their work where they were. The hardest and most unpromising field was not to be passed by. So every one of Christ's workers is to begin where he is. In our own families may be souls hungry for sympathy, starving for the bread of life. There may be children to be trained for Christ. There are heathen at our very doors. Let us do faithfully the work that is nearest. Then let our efforts be extended as far as God's hand may lead the way. The work of many may appear to be restricted by circumstances; but, wherever it is, if performed with faith and diligence it will be felt to the uttermost parts of the earth. Christ's work when upon earth appeared to be confined to a narrow field, but multitudes from all lands heard His message. God often uses the simplest means to accomplish the greatest results. It is His plan that every part of His work shall depend on every other part, as a wheel within a wheel, all acting in harmony. The humblest worker, moved by the Holy Spirit, will touch invisible chords, whose vibrations will ring to the ends of the earth, and make melody through eternal ages.

But the command, "Go ye into all the world," is not to be lost sight of. We are called upon to lift our eyes to the "regions beyond." Christ tears away the wall of partition, the dividing prejudice of nationality, and teaches a love for all the human family. He lifts men from the narrow circle which their selfishness prescribes; He abolishes all territorial lines and artificial distinctions of society. He makes no difference between neighbors and strangers, friends and enemies. He teaches us to look upon every needy soul as our brother, and the world as our field.

When the Saviour said, "Go, . . . teach all nations," He said also, "These signs shall follow them that believe; In My name shall they cast out devils; they shall speak with new tongues; they shall take up serpents; and if they drink any deadly thing, it shall not hurt them; they shall lay hands on the sick, and they shall recover." The promise is as far-reaching as the commission. Not that all the gifts are imparted to each believer. The Spirit divides "to every man severally as He will." 1 Cor. 12:11. But the gifts of the Spirit are promised to every believer according to his need for the Lord's work. The promise is just as strong and trustworthy now as in the days of the apostles. "These signs shall follow them that believe." This is the privilege of God's children, and faith should lay hold on all that it is possible to have as an indorsement of faith.

"They shall lay hands on the sick, and they shall recover." This world is a vast lazar house, but Christ came to heal the sick, to proclaim deliverance to the captives of Satan. He was in Himself health and strength. He imparted His life to the sick, the afflicted, those possessed of demons. He turned away none who came to receive His healing power. He knew that those who petitioned Him for help had brought disease upon themselves; yet He did not refuse to heal them. And when virtue from Christ entered into these poor souls, they were convicted of sin, and many were healed of their spiritual disease, as well as of their physical maladies. The gospel still possesses the same power, and why should we not today witness the same results?

Christ feels the woes of every sufferer. When evil spirits rend a human frame, Christ feels the curse. When fever is burning up the life current, He feels the agony. And He is just as willing to heal the sick now as when He was personally on earth. Christ's servants are His representatives, the channels for His working. He desires through them to exercise His healing power.

In the Saviour's manner of healing there were lessons for His disciples. On one occasion He anointed the eyes of a blind man with clay, and bade him, "Go, wash in the pool of Siloam. . . . He went his way therefore, and washed, and came seeing." John 9:7. The cure could be wrought only by the power of the Great Healer, yet Christ made use of the simple agencies of nature. While He did not give countenance to drug medication, He sanctioned the use of simple and natural remedies.

To many of the afflicted ones who received healing, Christ said, "Sin no more, lest a worse thing come unto thee." John 5:14. Thus He taught that disease is the result of violating God's laws, both natural and spiritual. The great misery in the world would not exist did men but live in harmony with the Creator's plan.

Christ had been the guide and teacher of ancient Israel, and He taught them that health is the reward of obedience to the laws of God. The Great Physician who healed the sick in Palestine had spoken to His people from the pillar of cloud, telling them what they must do, and what God would do for them. "If thou wilt diligently hearken to the voice of the Lord thy God," He said, "and wilt do that which is right in His sight, and wilt give ear to His commandments, and keep all His statutes, I will put none of these diseases upon thee, which I have brought upon the Egyptians: for I am the Lord that healeth thee." Ex. 15:26. Christ gave to Israel definite instruction in regard to their habits of life, and He assured them, "The Lord will take away from thee all sickness." Deut. 7:15. When they fulfilled the conditions, the promise was verified to them. "There was not one feeble person among their tribes." Ps. 105:37.

These lessons are for us. There are conditions to be observed by all who would preserve health. All should learn what these conditions are. The Lord is not pleased with ignorance in regard to His laws, either natural or spiritual. We are to be workers together with God for the restoration of health to the body as well as to the soul. {DA 824.4}

And we should teach others how to preserve and to recover health. For the sick we should use the remedies which God has provided in nature, and we should point them to Him who alone can restore. It is our work to present the sick and suffering to Christ in the arms of our faith. We should teach them to believe in the Great Healer. We should lay hold on His promise, and pray for the manifestation of His power.

The very essence of the gospel is restoration, and the Saviour would have us bid the sick, the hopeless, and the afflicted take hold upon His strength.

The power of love was in all Christ's healing, and only by partaking of that love, through faith, can we be instruments for His work. If we neglect to link ourselves in divine connection with Christ, the current of life-giving energy cannot flow in rich streams from us to the people. There were places where the Saviour Himself could not do many mighty works because of their unbelief. So now unbelief separates the church from her divine Helper. Her hold upon eternal realities is weak. By her lack of faith, God is disappointed, and robbed of His glory.

It is in doing Christ's work that the church has the promise of His presence. Go teach all nations, He said; "and, lo, I am with you alway, even unto the end of the world." To take His yoke is one of the first conditions of receiving His power. The very life of the church depends upon her faithfulness in fulfilling the Lord's commission. To neglect this work is surely to invite spiritual feebleness and decay. Where there is no active labor for others, love wanes, and faith grows dim.

Christ intends that His ministers shall be educators of the church in gospel work. They are to teach the people how to seek and save the lost. But is this the work they are doing? Alas, how many are toiling to fan the spark of life in a church that is ready to die! How many churches are tended like sick lambs by those who ought to be seeking for the lost sheep! And all the time millions upon millions without Christ are perishing.

Divine love has been stirred to its unfathomable depths for the sake of men, and angels marvel to behold in the recipients of so great love a mere surface gratitude. Angels marvel at man's shallow appreciation of the love of God. Heaven stands indignant at the neglect shown to the souls of men. Would we know how Christ regards it? How would a father and mother feel, did they know that their child, lost in the cold and the snow, had been passed by, and left to perish, by those who might have saved it? Would they not be terribly grieved, wildly indignant? Would they not denounce those murderers with wrath hot as their tears, intense as their love? The sufferings of every man are the sufferings of God's child, and those who reach out no helping hand to their perishing fellow beings provoke His righteous anger. This is the wrath of the Lamb. To those who claim fellowship with Christ, yet have been indifferent to the needs of their fellow men, He will declare in the great Judgment day, "I know you not whence ye are; depart from Me, all ye workers of iniquity." Luke 13:27.

In the commission to His disciples, Christ not only outlined their work, but gave them their message. Teach the people, He said, "to observe all things whatsoever I have commanded you." The disciples were to teach what Christ had taught. That which He had spoken, not only in person, but through all the prophets and teachers of the Old Testament, is here included. Human teaching is shut out. There is no place for tradition, for man's theories and conclusions, or for church legislation. No laws ordained by ecclesiastical authority are included in the commission. None of these are Christ's servants to teach. "The law and the prophets," with the record of His own words and deeds, are the treasure committed to the disciples to be given to the world. Christ's name is their watchword, their badge of distinction, their bond of union, the authority for their course of action, and the source of their success. Nothing that does not bear His superscription is to be recognized in His kingdom.

The gospel is to be presented, not as a lifeless theory, but as a living force to change the life. God desires that the receivers of His grace shall be witnesses to its power. Those whose course has been most offensive to Him He freely accepts; when they repent, He imparts to them His divine Spirit, places them in the highest positions of trust, and sends them forth into the camp of the disloyal to proclaim His boundless mercy. He would have His servants bear testimony to the fact that through His grace men may possess Christlikeness of character, and may rejoice in the assurance of His great love. He would have us bear testimony to the fact that He cannot be satisfied until the human race are reclaimed and reinstated in their holy privileges as

His sons and daughters.

In Christ is the tenderness of the shepherd, the affection of the parent, and the matchless grace of the compassionate Saviour. His blessings He presents in the most alluring terms. He is not content merely to announce these blessings; He presents them in the most attractive way, to excite a desire to possess them. So His servants are to present the riches of the glory of the unspeakable Gift. The wonderful love of Christ will melt and subdue hearts, when the mere reiteration of doctrines would accomplish nothing. "Comfort ye, comfort ye My people, saith your God." "O Zion, that bringest good tidings, get thee up into the high mountain; O Jerusalem, that bringest good tidings, lift up thy voice with strength; lift it up, be not afraid; say unto the cities of Judah, Behold your God! . . . He shall feed His flock like a shepherd: He shall gather the lambs with His arm, and carry them in His bosom." Isa. 40:1, 9-11. Tell the people of Him who is "the Chiefest among ten thousand," and the One "altogether lovely." The Song of Solomon 5:10, 16. Words alone cannot tell it. Let it be reflected in the character and manifested in the life. Christ is sitting for His portrait in every disciple. Every one God has predestinated to be "conformed to the image of His Son." Rom. 8:29. In every one Christ's long-suffering love, His holiness, meekness, mercy, and truth are to be manifested to the world.

The first disciples went forth preaching the word. They revealed Christ in their lives. And the Lord worked with them, "confirming the word with signs following." Mark 16:20. These disciples prepared themselves for their work. Before the day of Pentecost they met together, and put away all differences. They were of one accord. They believed Christ's promise that the blessing would be given, and they prayed in faith. They did not ask for a blessing for themselves merely; they were weighted with the burden for the salvation of souls. The gospel was to be carried to the uttermost parts of the earth, and they claimed the endowment of power that Christ had promised. Then it was that the Holy Spirit was poured out, and thousands were converted in a day.

So it may be now. Instead of man's speculations, let the word of God be preached. Let Christians put away their dissensions, and give themselves to God for the saving of the lost. Let them in faith ask for the blessing, and it will come. The outpouring of the Spirit in apostolic days was the "former rain," and glorious was the result. But the "latter rain" will be more abundant. Joel 2:23.

All who consecrate soul, body, and spirit to God will be constantly receiving a new endowment of physical and mental power. The inexhaustible supplies of heaven are at their command. Christ gives them the breath of His own spirit, the life of His own life. The Holy Spirit puts forth its highest energies to work in heart and mind. The grace of God enlarges and multiplies their faculties, and every perfection of the divine nature comes to their assistance in the work of saving souls. Through co-operation with Christ they are complete in Him, and in their human weakness they are enabled to do the deeds of Omnipotence.

The Saviour longs to manifest His grace and stamp His character on the whole world. It is His purchased possession, and He desires to make men free, and pure, and holy. Though Satan works to hinder this purpose, yet through the blood shed for the world there are triumphs to be achieved that will bring glory to God and the Lamb. Christ will not be satisfied till the victory is complete, and "He shall see of the travail of His soul, and shall be satisfied." Isa. 53:11. All the nations of the earth shall hear the gospel of His grace. Not all will receive His grace; but "a seed shall serve Him; it shall be accounted to the Lord for a generation." Ps. 22:30. "The kingdom and dominion, and the greatness of the kingdom under the whole heaven, shall be given to the people of the saints of the Most High," and "the earth shall be full of the knowledge of the Lord, as the waters cover the sea." "So shall they fear the name of the Lord from the west, and His glory from the rising of the sun." Dan. 7:27; Isa. 11:9; 59:19.

"How beautiful upon the mountains are the feet of him that bringeth good tidings, that publisheth peace; that bringeth good tidings of good, that publisheth salvation; that saith unto Zion, Thy God reigneth! . . . Break forth into joy, sing together, ye waste places: . . . for the Lord hath comforted His people. . . . The Lord hath made bare His holy arm in the eyes of all the nations; and all the ends of the earth shall see the salvation of our God." Isa. 52:7-10.

FOURTEEN

"TO MY FATHER, AND YOUR FATHER"

The time had come for Christ to ascend to His Father's throne. As a divine conqueror He was about to return with the trophies of victory to the heavenly courts. Before His death He had declared to His Father, "I have finished the work which Thou gavest Me to do." John 17:4. After His resurrection He tarried on earth for a season, that His disciples might become familiar with Him in His risen and glorified body. Now He was ready for the leave-taking. He had authenticated the fact that He was a living Saviour. His disciples need no longer associate Him with the tomb. They could think of Him as glorified before the heavenly universe.

As the place of His ascension, Jesus chose the spot so often hallowed by His presence while He dwelt among men. Not Mount Zion, the place of David's city, not Mount Moriah, the temple site, was to be thus honored. There Christ had been mocked and rejected. There the waves of mercy, still returning in a stronger tide of love, had been beaten back by hearts as hard as rock. Thence Jesus, weary and heart-burdened, had gone forth to find rest in the Mount of Olives. The holy Shekinah, in departing from the first temple, had stood upon the eastern mountain, as if loath to forsake the chosen city; so Christ stood upon Olivet, with yearning heart overlooking Jerusalem. The groves and glens of the mountain had been consecrated by His prayers and tears. Its steeps had echoed the triumphant shouts of the multitude that proclaimed Him king. On its sloping descent He had found a home with Lazarus at Bethany. In the garden of Gethsemane at its foot He had prayed and agonized alone. From this mountain He was to ascend to heaven. Upon its summit His feet will rest when He shall come again. Not as a man of sorrows, but as a glorious and triumphant king He will stand upon Olivet, while Hebrew hallelujahs mingle with Gentile hosannas, and the voices of the redeemed as a mighty host shall swell the acclamation, "Crown Him Lord of all!

Now with the eleven disciples Jesus made His way toward the mountain. As they passed through the gate of Jerusalem, many wondering eyes looked upon the little company, led by One whom a few weeks before the rulers had condemned and crucified. The disciples knew not that this was to be their last interview with their Master. Jesus spent the time in conversation with them, repeating His former instruction. As they approached Gethsemane, He paused, that they might call to mind the lessons He had given them on the night of His great agony. Again He looked upon the vine by which He had then represented the union of His church with Himself and His Father; again He repeated the truths He had then unfolded. All around Him were reminders of His unrequited love. Even the disciples who were so dear to His heart, had, in the hour of His humiliation, reproached and forsaken Him.

Christ had sojourned in the world for thirty-three years; He had endured its scorn, insult, and mockery; He had been rejected and crucified. Now, when about to ascend to His throne of glory,—as He reviews the ingratitude of the people He came to save,—will He not withdraw from them His sympathy and love? Will not His affections be centered upon that realm where He is appreciated, and where sinless angels wait to do His bidding? No; His promise to those loved ones whom He leaves on earth is, "I am with you alway, even unto the end of the world." Matt. 28:20.

Upon reaching the Mount of Olives, Jesus led the way across the summit, to the vicinity of Bethany. Here He paused, and the disciples gathered about Him. Beams of light seemed to radiate from His countenance as He looked lovingly upon them. He upbraided them not for their faults and failures; words of the deepest tenderness were the last that fell upon their ears from the lips of their Lord. With hands outstretched in blessing, and as if in assurance of His protecting care, He slowly ascended from among them, drawn heavenward by a power stronger than any earthly attraction. As He passed upward, the awe-stricken disciples looked with straining eyes for the last glimpse of their ascending Lord. A cloud of glory hid Him from their sight; and the words came back to them as the cloudy chariot of angels received Him, "Lo, I am with you alway, even unto the end of the world." At the same time there floated down to them the sweetest and most joyous music from the angel choir.

While the disciples were still gazing upward, voices addressed them which sounded like richest music. They turned, and saw two angels in the form of men, who spoke to them, saying, "Ye men of Galilee, why stand ye gazing up into heaven? this same Jesus, which is taken up from you into heaven, shall so come in like manner as ye have seen Him go into heaven."

These angels were of the company that had been waiting in a shining cloud to escort Jesus to His heavenly home. The most exalted of the angel throng, they were the two who had come to the tomb at Christ's resurrection, and they had been with Him throughout His life on earth. With eager desire all heaven had waited for the end of His tarrying in a world marred by the curse of sin. The time had now come for the heavenly universe to receive their King. Did not the two angels long to join the throng that welcomed Jesus? But in sympathy and love for those whom He had left, they waited to give them comfort. "Are they not all ministering spirits, sent forth to minister for them who shall be heirs of salvation?" Heb. 1:14.

Christ had ascended to heaven in the form of humanity. The disciples had beheld the cloud receive Him. The same Jesus who had walked and talked and prayed with them; who had broken bread with them; who had been with them in their boats on the lake; and who had that very day toiled with them up the ascent of Olivet,—the same Jesus had now gone to share His Father's throne. And the angels had assured them that the very One whom they had seen go up into heaven, would come again even as He had ascended. He will come "with clouds; and every eye shall see Him." "The Lord Himself shall descend from heaven with a shout, with the voice of the Archangel, and with the trump of God: and the dead in Christ shall rise." "The Son of man shall come in His glory, and all the holy angels with Him, then shall He sit upon the throne of His glory." Rev. 1:7; 1 Thess. 4:16; Matt. 25:31. Thus will be fulfilled the Lord's own promise to His disciples: "If I go and prepare a place for you, I will come again, and receive you unto Myself; that where I am, there ye may be also." John 14:3. Well might the disciples rejoice in the hope of their Lord's return.

When the disciples went back to Jerusalem, the people looked upon them with amazement. After the trial and crucifixion of Christ, it had been thought that they would appear downcast and ashamed. Their enemies expected to see upon their faces an expression of sorrow and defeat. Instead of this there was only gladness and triumph. Their faces were aglow with a happiness not born of earth. They did not mourn over disappointed hopes, but were full of praise and thanksgiving to God. With rejoicing they told the wonderful story of Christ's resurrection and His ascension to heaven, and their testimony was received by many.

The disciples no longer had any distrust of the future. They knew that Jesus was in heaven, and that His sympathies were with them still. They knew that they had a friend at the throne of God, and they were eager to present their requests to the Father in the name of Jesus. In solemn awe they bowed in prayer, repeating the assurance, "Whatsoever ye shall ask the Father in My name, He will give it you. Hitherto have ye asked nothing in My name: ask, and ye shall receive, that your joy may be full." John 16:23, 24. They extended the hand of faith higher and higher, with the mighty argument, "It is Christ that died, yea rather, that is risen again, who is even at the right hand of God, who also maketh intercession for us." Rom. 8:34. And Pentecost brought them fullness of joy in the presence of the Comforter, even as Christ had promised.

All heaven was waiting to welcome the Saviour to the celestial courts. As He ascended, He led the way, and the multitude of captives set free at His resurrection followed. The heavenly host, with shouts and acclamations of praise and celestial song, attended the joyous train.

As they drew near to the city of God, the challenge is given by the escorting angels,—

> "Lift up your heads, O ye gates;
> And be ye lift up, ye everlasting doors;
> And the King of glory shall come in."

Joyfully the waiting sentinels respond,—

> "Who is this King of glory?"

This they say, not because they know not who He is, but because they would hear the answer of exalted praise,—

> "The Lord strong and mighty,
> The Lord mighty in battle!
> Lift up your heads, O ye gates;
> Even lift them up, ye everlasting doors;
> And the King of glory shall come in."

Again is heard the challenge, "Who is this King of glory?" for the angels never weary of hearing His name exalted. The escorting angels make reply,—

> "The Lord of hosts;
> He is the King of glory." Ps. 24:7-10.

Then the portals of the city of God are opened wide, and the angelic throng sweep through the gates amid a burst of rapturous music.

There is the throne, and around it the rainbow of promise. There are cherubim and seraphim. The commanders of the angel hosts, the sons of God, the representatives of the unfallen worlds, are assembled. The heavenly council before which Lucifer had accused God and His Son, the representatives of those sinless realms over which Satan had thought to establish his dominion,—all are there to welcome the Redeemer. They are eager to celebrate His triumph and to glorify their King.

But He waves them back. Not yet; He cannot now receive the coronet of glory and the royal robe. He enters into the presence of His Father. He points to His wounded head, the pierced side, the marred feet; He lifts His hands, bearing the print of nails. He points to the tokens of His triumph; He presents to God the wave sheaf, those raised with Him as representatives of that great multitude who shall come forth from the grave at His second coming. He approaches the Father, with whom there is joy over one sinner that repents; who rejoices over one with singing. Before the foundations of the earth were laid, the Father and the Son had united in a covenant to redeem man if he should be overcome by Satan. They had clasped Their hands in a solemn pledge that Christ should become the surety for the human race. This pledge Christ has fulfilled. When upon the cross He cried out, "It is finished," He addressed the Father. The compact had been fully carried out. Now He declares: Father, it is finished. I have done Thy will, O My God. I have completed the work of redemption. If Thy justice is satisfied, "I will that they also, whom Thou hast given Me, be with Me where I am." John 19:30; 17:24.

The voice of God is heard proclaiming that justice is satisfied. Satan is vanquished. Christ's toiling, struggling ones on earth are "accepted in the Beloved." Eph. 1:6. Before the heavenly angels and the representatives of unfallen worlds, they are declared justified. Where He is, there His church shall be. "Mercy and truth are met together; righteousness and peace have kissed each other." Ps. 85:10. The Father's arms encircle His Son, and the word is given, "Let all the angels of God worship Him." Heb. 1:6.

With joy unutterable, rulers and principalities and powers acknowledge the supremacy of the Prince of life. The angel host prostrate themselves before Him, while the glad shout fills all the courts of heaven, "Worthy is the Lamb that was slain to receive power, and riches, and wisdom, and strength, and honor, and glory, and blessing." Rev. 5:12.

Songs of triumph mingle with the music from angel harps, till heaven seems to overflow with joy and praise. Love has conquered. The lost is found. Heaven rings with voices in lofty strains proclaiming, "Blessing, and honor, and glory, and power, be unto Him that sitteth upon the throne, and unto the Lamb forever and ever." Rev. 5:13.

❦

From that scene of heavenly joy, there comes back to us on earth the echo of Christ's own wonderful words, "I ascend unto My Father, and your Father; and to My God, and your God." John 20:17. The family of heaven and the family of earth are one. For us our Lord ascended, and for us He lives. "Wherefore He is able also to save them to the uttermost that come unto God by Him, seeing He ever liveth to make intercession for them." Heb. 7:25.

THE REAL PASSION PLAY

Mel Gibson's, "The Passion of the Christ," touches a vital nerve. For many it is a deeply moving spiritual experience. For others the violent portrayal of Christ's brutal suffering is too great for them to emotionally handle.

Perhaps you have seen the film or maybe you haven't. What's the meaning of it all? Why all this horror? Was Jesus simply a martyr dying for a good cause? Why is the cross at the heart of Christianity?

There is something beyond the excruciating pain Jesus experienced on the cross. There is something more significant than the immensity of His physical suffering. There is something more than strong-armed, muscular Roman soldiers driving jagged nails through tender flesh. There is something more than a Roman lash embedded with fragments of metal ripping out hunks of flesh from His lacerated back. As horrible as His physical suffering really was, if that is all we see happening on Golgotha's mountain we have really missed the meaning of it all.

The blood that oozes from His temple, spurts from His hands and flows from His feet, speaks of a God who would rather endure unbearable pain Himself than have one of His children lost. The cross reveals, to a waiting world and a watching universe, the immensity of God's love. For you see, a rebel angel has challenged God's government. He has claimed God is arbitrary, cruel, and unjust. He declared, God exacts love but does not give it. The cross reveals his lie. It unmasks his delusion. It reveals his cunning falsehood.

The essence of Calvary's meaning is not the first death. It is the second. The Bible teaches there are two deaths. The physical death, which everyone of us must die because we are born into a fallen world. (Romans 5:12) The second death is the eternal death which is the ultimate consequence of sin. (Romans 6:23)

When Jesus died on the cross, He experienced much more than physical death. The apostle Paul asserts, "He who knew no sin became sin for us."(2 Cor 5:21) He then adds, "Cursed is everyone who hangs upon the tree." (Gal 3:13) On the cross Jesus experienced the lostness of humanity. The guilt of sin crushed out His life. Suspended between heaven and earth, Jesus experienced the Father's condemnation against sin. In every fiber of His being, in every nerve and every tissue of His body, in every tinge of emotion – physically – mentally – spiritually, Jesus experienced what it would be like to be lost. Lostness is eternal separation from God in total annihilation. It is to be God forsaken. Sin is so horrible it separates sinners from God forever.

Jesus who existed with the Father, from all eternity, went through the wrenching agony of having His heart torn apart. Bearing the guilt and condemnation of our sins. He was willing to be lost forever, if that is what it took to save us forever.

As the federal head of the entire human race, He took upon Himself willingly and voluntarily all the condemnation of sin.

He was willing to be separated from the Father eternally so I could live with the Father eternally. He was condemned for my sins in which He had no share so I could receive His righteousness in which I had no share.

He wore the crown of thorns so I could wear the crown of glory. He hung on a bloody tree, so I could eat from the tree of life. His hands were spiked to a wooden bar, so mine can clutch the hands of a loving Father. He died the death that was mine so I could live the life that was His.

There is no other love like this in all of the universe. He loves you too much to let you go without putting up a fight. He is reaching out to you right now. He is speaking to your heart this very moment. The Christ who died did not remain in the darkness of the tomb. He is alive. He resurrected from the dead, and He longs for you to live with

Him forever.

He invites you to come to Him right now. Come with all of your guilt. Come with all of your heavy burdens. Come with all of your sin. Come with all of your heartache and pain. Come and give Him your life today. Come and receive His grace, His mercy, His pardon, His forgiveness, His strength, and His power. Come and receive the most wonderful gift of all — "Eternal life through Christ Jesus our Lord."

Why not pray this prayer.

Dear Lord,

I come to you right now. Thank you for your incredible, incomprehensible love revealed on Calvary's cross. Thank you for bearing the guilt of my sins there. Just now, I give you my life and accept your gift of eternal life in Jesus name.

Amen

Mark A. Finley
World Evangelist
It Is Written Television
Simi Valley, California

THE ACCOUNT THAT YOU HAVE JUST READ IS ONLY PART OF THE STORY.

For more of the story of Jesus, you are invited to
contact the publisher for other inspired books
written by E.G. White and more.

The Desire of Ages
The complete book on the life of Jesus.

In God We Trust 9/11 Memorial Edition (Steps To Christ).
Developing a relationship with Jesus.
Translated into 140 languages. Over 100 million in print.

The Great Controversy
A companion book dealing with prophecy.

Ministry of Healing, Counsels on Diet & Foods
Books for your health.

The Greatest Sermon Ever Preached
(Thoughts from the Mount of Blessings)
Lessons and teachings from the Beatitudes of Christ.

Christ's Object Lessons
Teachings on the parables of Jesus.

Bible Readings for the Home
A topical study of the Bible in question & answer format.
More than one million sold.

In the Bible, John states at the end of his book about Jesus; "And there
are also many other things which Jesus did, the which, if they should
be written every one, I suppose that even the world itself could not
contain the books that should be written, Amen." John 21:25

The publisher of this book is convinced that the inspired writings of
E.G.White are some of those books of which John speaks.
                                              —HOMEWARD PUBLISHING

I am interested in the books listed.
Please furnish me further information.

❏ **The Desire of Ages**

❏ **In God We Trust**

❏ **The Great Controversy**

❏ **Ministry of Healing**

❏ **Counsels on Diet & Foods**

❏ **The Greatest Sermon Ever Preached**

❏ **Christ's Object Lessons**

❏ **Bible Readings for the Home**

Please print the following information.

Name _____

Address _____

City _____

State _____ *Zip* _____

Please mail this completed coupon to:
HOMEWARD PUBLISHING
P.O. BOX 111, EARLTON, NY 12058
www.passionoftheages.com
eMail: shorter@mhonline.net

NEED PRAYER?
www.safetv.org

SAFE TV
HAS A PASSION
FOR SOULS

The Safe TV Channel® provides you and your family with Safe Television For All Ages®. Anyone of any age can watch it at any time. Our greatest **PASSION** is to share the love of our Lord and Savior Jesus Christ. That is why we provide weekly, inspirational programming that uplifts God, Family and Country – programs such as:

Amazing Facts
American Religious Town Hall
Breath of Life
Esta' Escrito
Everlasting Gospel
It Is Written
New Perceptions
Purely Music
The Carter Report
United Prison Ministries, Int'l
Voice of Prophecy
Windows of Hope
And more!

For information on how you may receive Safe TV® via satellite in your home: Please call **Safe TV® at 1-888-777-9392** or visit our web site at **www.safetv.org.**

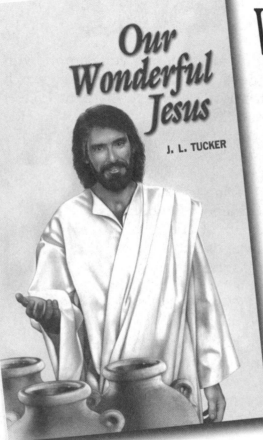